WOKE OR NOT?

A GUIDE TO WOKE FOR OLDER PEOPLE

NINA THOM

ISBN: 978-0-6459544-0-1 (Paperback)

ISBN: 978-0-6459544-1-8 (Ebook)

CONTENTS

INTRODUCTION

Welcome to Woke or Not?: A Woke Guide For Older People

Whether new to the woke conversation or seeking a deeper understanding, this guide will be an accessible and informative resource for those curious about the "woke phenomena" and will answer all those questions: What does "woke" mean? Who are "the Woke"? What is this enigmatic "Woke Culture"? And is being woke a force for good, or does it come with its own challenges?

"Woke" is a word whose ordinary meaning is to signal "sleep is done," but in modern times, it has adopted new and multiple meanings. Today woke is a catchy buzzword, a metaphor for social justice awareness, and an adjective for describing people, their culture, and ideologies. Yet it is also a paradoxical noun, capable of being a badge of honor or a stinging insult.

Wokeism originates in a progressive political ideology that found its roots in the late 1800s. It has evolved into a catalyst for pivotal racial and gender reforms that persist today. The intriguing history of the slang use of the term traces back to the black community in the 1930s. The rallying cry "Stay Woke" was reignited by determined black activists in 2013, echoing the historic civil rights movement, to protest against police brutality during the rise of the Black Lives Matter Movement. In a decade of rapid expansion of social media platforms, woke gained significant traction in Gen Z popular culture and online public debate, inspiring other social justice issues such as the Me Too and Climate Justice Movements.

However, woke faced its own controversies when weaponized through an online vigilante practice called "Cancel Culture." It became a divisive social concept, co-opted by "good faith" and "bad faith actors," celebrities, politicians, journalists, and influencers in the public eye. Woke became a battleground, accused of threatening free speech, family values, democracy, and even being a religious cult. Although Wokeism has been the driving force for anti-racism, anti-sexism, and gender reforms, in an ironic twist, it is now scrutinized by anti-woke critics for its negative impact on education and politics, which has led to it being branded the new "evil" in a media-fuelled "War on Woke."

Despite these challenges, Wokeism endures as an integral part of progressive politics and culture that is not easily dismissed. This guide draws on research and data from various sources: academics, authors, journalists, social and political analysts, and educators, to unravel the intricacies of Woke, a concept that most people have heard of but few really understand.

1

DEFINING WOKE

Language is a dynamic phenomenon, and "woke" is a striking example. As linguistic expert John McWhorter points out: "spoken language is even more fluid than written language (McWhorter, 2021b)." Woke has been used in multiple ways over its 100-year history: from a codified warning for black people to stay alert to racial injustice to a metaphor for reverse racism against whites and everything between.

In 2020, journalist Aja Romano wrote, "As use of the word spreads, what people actually mean by "woke" seems less clear than ever (Romano, 2020)." While woke first appeared as a slang word in the 1930s, it wasn't until 2017 it was legitimized in the Merriam-Webster online dictionary (Merriam-Webster, 2022) as an adjective that means:

- Aware of and actively attentive to important societal facts and issues, especially issues of racial and social justice (being woke or wokest)
- often used in contexts that suggest someone's expressed beliefs about such matters are not backed

with genuine concern or action (performative or fake woke)

- reflecting the attitudes of woke people (wokeness)
- disapproving: politically liberal (as in matters of racial and social justice), especially in a way that is considered unreasonable or extreme (Wokeism)

To better understand the more nuanced meanings of woke will involve exploring how the word evolved from a simple past participle of the verb "to wake" to become a noun that defines the progressive political ideology and cultural phenomena called "Wokeism."

ORIGINS OF THE WORD WOKE

A Metaphor for Being Alert to Racism

After major social reforms in America during the Progressive Era from the 1890s to the 1920s, there was an emergence of Black nationalist activism in the 1930s through leaders such as Jamaican-born Marcus Garvey. He used the metaphor "wake up" to urge black people to be awake from the mental slumber that had resulted from centuries of slavery and racist oppression (Moses, 2020).

A Smithsonian recording of the 1930s protest song, "*Scottsboro Boys*, captured black singer Huddie Ledbetter's quiet warning to his audience, "Best stay woke, keep their eyes open (Smithsonian Folksways Collection, 2015)". Romano writes, "Lead Belly uses 'stay woke' in explicit association with Black Americans' need to be aware of racially motivated threats and the potential dangers of white America (Romano, 2020)."

Being Alert to Social Injustice

In 1942, journalist J. Saunders Redding captured the political use of the term as a metaphor for the growing union pushback by African Americans against social injustice. A black unionist tells him, "Waking up is a damn sight harder than going to sleep, but we'll stay woke up longer" (Redding, 1942).

Civil Rights Activism

Although the term woke doesn't specifically appear to have been used during the volatile period of Civil Rights Activism in the 1960s, the use of the metaphor "wake up" as a call to black Americans to "stop ignoring racial oppression and take action" is a common theme in many powerful speeches by black activists Dr. Martin Luther King, and Malcolm X.

Harlem Slang for Well-informed

By the 1960s, woke had become an African American Vernacular Expression (AAVE) for being "with it" or well-informed and aware in the political context. Around that time, William Melvin Kelley, an African American novelist, was the first to codify the term in a *New York Times* article titled: *"If You're Woke, You Dig It: the most common phrases that you may hear in Harlem,"* signifying the word woke had reached mainstream media (Kelley, 1962). Kelley is called the "godfather of woke" by journalist Elijah Watson in one of his articles in *The Origin of Woke* series, which describes Kelley's prophetic insight about black slang concerning its invention, reinvention, and appropriation by white people (Watson, 2017).

A Reminder to Stay Aware

The term woke briefly reappeared as a metaphor for "awareness of social issues" in the 1972 Barry Beckham play "Garvey Lives" with one of the characters saying: "I been sleeping all my life. And now that Mr. Garvey done woke me up, I'm gon stay woke (Beckham, 2017)."

Reassuring Invocation

Journalist Kashana Cauley recalls how the phrase "stay woke" was a life vest for a young black teen growing up in a 1990s white society. Conversations with her parents to be vigilant against racial discrimination ended by invoking this phrase. "This is the version of *woke* that I grew up with: a call to study and act against anti-black oppression," she says (Cauley, 2019).

Deandre Miles-Hercules, a black linguistics expert, explains how woke was initially used as a code, like many slang words, as a "linguistic subterfuge" for black people to speak indirectly against white racism and brutality (Miles-Hercules & Muwwakkil, 2021).

REINVENTING WOKE

The Spread of Woke Through Music

Watson's 2018 article describes how music helped pass the word woke "from the streets of Harlem to the West Coast and eventually into the airwaves for mass consumption (Watson, 2018)." By 2008, the song titled *'I Stay Woke,'* written by Georgia Muldrow and rereleased by R&B artist Erykah Badu, brought the term to a broader black audience. The song inspired the widespread use of the phrase "stay woke" through Black social media to highlight racial injustice. It took on a more specific meaning for Muldrow and others: "To be woke is to be black" (Watson, 2018).

A Rallying Cry for Black Activism

The turning point occurred shortly after, as "Stay Woke" erupted as a rallying cry for the Black Lives Matter (BLM) movement in 2013. It became an "infectious" viral hashtag as #Stay Woke became a call to action, urging people to go beyond being aware and get personally engaged in the fight against systemic racism against black people and police brutality (BLM, 2019). As Watson explains: "Woke was simultaneously a cool and militant descriptor for our experience, a word that channeled our reality into something empowering (Watson, 2018)."

Woke Becomes the "Buzzword"

Woke continued to be used in various contexts related to black activism, including protests, social media, and music. It became the buzzword that described "woke culture," "wokeness," and "woke people," and represented a progressive ideology called "Wokeism," a catch-all word to describe social justice movements that challenged: racism, sexism, gender inequality, environmental damage, indigenous rights, wealth disparity, and disability discrimination.

"Being Woke" was considered a status symbol as Hollywood celebrities joined the rising wave of social activism during the Me Too movement. Watson describes this trend "of liberal white people of all ages co-opting woke and treating it like a badge of honor (Watson, 2020)," foreshadowing how performative woke would become in the following years.

Performative Woke

Wokeism was no longer just about advocacy but was commodified as a marketing brand. Social media influencers, and corporations, began to realize its consumer appeal, and the use of symbols, slogans, and social justice rhetoric began to take on a superficial tone. As a virtuous and socially responsible person or company, self-promotion on social media became prioritized over genuinely engaging in woke activism. These actions were readily dubbed as "virtue signaling" and "woke-washing" and started to dominate the conversation around social justice, drawing criticism for being performative gestures that undermined meaningful change.

Weaponized Woke

As online political activism flourished, Wokeism became driven by language rules known as "political correctness" or "PC" culture. Specific social rules were used to moderate public discourse. They were intended to promote more inclusive and safe spaces for marginalized people. Those who disregarded this social code were quickly "called out" or "canceled" through public shaming and cultural boycotts.

The practice, predominately associated as part of the Woke movement, started as an effective way for everyday people to bring accountability to individuals and organizations that displayed problematic behavior but evolved into a pervasive "Cancel Culture" that became increasingly punitive or retaliatory. Woke was weaponized to censor various views and opinions, sometimes stifling free speech and causing division.

Ironic Woke

Performative activism and Cancel Culture peaked during the pandemic, where overzealous online language policing and "virtue signaling" gained the attention of quick-witted comedians and disapproving conservatives. They pounced on the inconsistencies and hypocrisy appearing in woke spaces. "Woke" became an ironic term of derision to mock the exaggerated "political correctness" and superficial aspects of Wokeism (Hampton & Kircher, 2021).

Woke as a Derogatory Slur

Online exchanges on social justice issues became increasingly hostile and focused on character assassination rather than healthy debates. "Cancel culture" was rampant, and being Woke shifted from the heroic to the divisive. Wokeness was increasingly associated with online bullying, abuse, and harassment that occasionally spilled into real-life attacks. The mainstream media portrayal of woke became nastier, and using the term woke as a derogatory slur became more common (CBS News, 2020b).

The Rise of the Anti-woke

In the wake of the 2016 presidential election, far-right conservative critics became more emboldened to challenge all aspects of Wokeism. They mounted a strong pushback against progressive social reforms, with some arguing that wokeness was a threat to free speech, intellectual diversity, and the democratic process. This increased political polarization and inspired a group of vocal right-wing conservatives called the Alternative Right, or Alt-right, to mount a campaign of white nationalist, religious conservatism. The goals of Wokeism were dismissed as

Anti-American, and it was targeted as a real threat to freedom and the "American way of life" (Harmon, 2022).

Woke is the New Evil

The concerns of Conservatives and Moderates, many of who were parents, were primarily focused on how Critical Race Theory and gender identity reforms were being introduced into elementary schools. They considered these progressive initiatives a threat to the healthy development of their children, highlighting their fears that Wokeism eroded accepted traditional family values, distorted their opinions on gender and race, and negatively impacted psychological health. Wokeism itself came under attack in what has been dubbed the "Woke Culture War."

Wokeism, rather than anti-racism or anti-discrimination, became their target. Being woke was a label that stereotyped Progressives as narrow-minded, arrogant, hypocritical, bigoted, and anti-American for supporting these controversial social reforms. Gradually, as momentum gathered in the wake of the 2020 election, Alt-right resentment of Wokeism escalated, and it was stigmatized as the new "evil" threatening American democracy.

THE FALL OF WOKE

Watson sees woke, "like anything created by black people," as a phrase appropriated by the masses (Watson, 2018). Deberry says it is another example of white people's appropriation of black culture and the subsequent "erasure of the people who invented it (Deberry, 2021)." While Wokeism peaked in popularity in the 2020s, woke is no longer in vogue as a term symbolizing black activism. However, the ongoing ferocity of resistance toward Wokeism signifies that its fundamental advocacy principles are still alive in many aspects of American society as a pervasive progressive influence.

Wokeism or Wokeness is complex and highly nuanced, and woke has shifted in meaning and use: It's controversial, misused, and misunderstood. The following chapters will define Woke Culture and the evolution of Wokeism's connection with progressive ideologies and how they underpin various social justice movements, political systems, education, the arts, media, and the corporate world today.

2

WHAT IS WOKE CULTURE?

At its core, the goals of Woke Culture, or Wokeism, are driven by a desire to raise awareness and promote greater equity and social justice. One fundamental tenet of Wokeism promoted by many social justice activists such as Esmeralda Simmons, Melanie Campbell, James Rucker, Lateefa Simon, Kimberlé Crenshaw, Tarana Bourke, Ibram X. Kendi, Susan Burtan, and Charlie Amaya Scott, is a belief in systemic oppression or the idea that certain groups are marginalized and systematically oppressed by existing power structures and institutions (Kendi, 2019). Wokeism aims to fight all forms of political, racial, and gender oppression and discrimination through activism and allyship; however, many principles are associated with Woke Culture.

DEFINING WOKE PRINCIPLES

Diversity

Diversity emphasizes recognizing and valuing the differences among individuals and communities, including race, ethnicity, gender, gender identity, sexual orientation, age, social class, physical ability or attributes, religion, ethical values, national origin, and political beliefs. Diversity involves promoting broader representation and participation of historically marginalized groups in all aspects of society, as well as creating more inclusive spaces and practices that accommodate a variety of perspectives and experiences.

Equity

Equity refers to the fair and just distribution of resources, opportunities, and privileges among individuals and groups in society. It emphasizes the importance of addressing historical and present-day inequalities that have resulted from multiple forms of discrimination. Equity seeks to level the playing field and recognizes that different people have different starting points, needs, and barriers. It aims to address systemic disadvantages and promote equality of outcomes by providing additional support, resources, and opportunities to those who have been historically marginalized.

Wokeism embodies the idea that everyone deserves an equal chance to succeed and thrive, regardless of background or identity. Specific policies and practices may need to be designed and implemented to achieve equity, such as affirmative action, inclusive education, accessible infrastructure, affordable healthcare, fair employment practices, and inclusive representation in decision-making processes.

Equality

Equality, as opposed to equity, refers to treating all individuals and groups fairly and impartially regardless of race, gender, socioeconomic status, or other protected characteristics. Equality means that everyone should have the same rights, opportunities, and access to resources and aims to eliminate systemic barriers and biases that prevent specific individuals or groups from enjoying the same benefits and opportunities as others. It promotes equal access to education, healthcare, employment, and other essential services.

However, some social justice advocates believe a "colorblind" approach to equality is still inherently biased. Although greatly improved, current social systems still disadvantage some racial and ethnic groups and a "race-conscious" approach to equality is promoted by many advocates as being fairer.

Inclusion

Inclusion means involvement and empowerment, where all people's inherent worth and dignity are recognized. An inclusive society promotes a sense of belonging and values those with different ideas, beliefs, cultural practices, and talents, regardless of their background or identity. This means creating environments welcoming and supportive of diverse perspectives and experiences and recognizing that exclusion and marginalization can take many forms and can cause harm to vulnerable people (Ahmed, 2012).

Representation

Representation refers to the fair and inclusive presence and participation of diverse individuals and groups in decision-making processes, institutions, and systems that impact their lives. It recognizes the importance of ensuring all voices are heard, perspectives are considered, and power is shared equitably. Representation addresses the historical underrepresentation and marginalization of specific communities. Representation is crucial for fostering a democratic and just society where all individuals' diverse needs, concerns, and aspirations are recognized, respected, and acted upon.

THE ROLE OF SOCIAL JUSTICE

Social justice is the central goal of Wokeism. It refers to the belief that all members of society should have access to the same rights, opportunities, and resources, regardless of their social, economic, or political status. It addresses and rectifies historic and current systemic inequalities, discrimination, and injustices based on various socio-economic factors and identities. It is founded on universal principles defined in the 1948 *United Nations Universal Declaration of Human Rights* (United Nations, 2023).

The fundamental objectives of social justice include:

- Equity and Fairness: eliminating discrimination and creating equal opportunities for all individuals.
- Human Rights: advocating for protecting and fulfilling fundamental rights and freedoms for all individuals.
- Inclusion and Diversity: recognizing and valuing diversity, promoting inclusivity, and respecting different identities, backgrounds, and experiences.
- Empowerment: aiming to give marginalized communities a voice, agency, and the power to advocate for their rights, shape their own destinies and build capacity.
- Collective Action: achieving meaningful change requires coordinated efforts and involves community organizing, activism, advocacy, and policy interventions to challenge systemic injustices and promote social transformation.

Social justice extends beyond individual actions and personal beliefs; it encompasses systemic changes and societal transformations that address the root causes of injustice. Social Justice is a broad concept that includes several areas of racial, gender, economic, and environmental justice.

Racial Justice

Racial justice refers to the pursuit of fairness, equality and the elimination of systemic racism and discrimination in all aspects of society. It seeks to promote anti-racism and address the historical and ongoing disparities, biases, and prejudices that impact marginalized racial and ethnic groups.

It aims to challenge and transform oppressive discriminative systems to ensure that all individuals, regardless of their racial or ethnic background, have equal opportunities, rights, and access to resources.

Some fundamental objectives of racial justice include:

- Equity and Equality for people of all races and ethnicities and addressing historical systems of racism and oppression.
- Anti-Racism: Actively opposing and combating racism in all its forms.
- Recognizing and respecting the diverse racial and ethnic identities within a society promotes inclusivity and cultural sensitivity and rejects stereotypes.
- Making structural changes in policies, laws, and practices to address systemic oppression and racism.
- Community engagement and empowerment.

Gender Justice

Gender justice refers to the pursuit of equality, fairness and eradicating gender-based discrimination, biases, and injustices in all spheres of life. It recognizes that gender norms, stereotypes, and power imbalances have historically marginalized and disadvantaged individuals based on their gender identity or expression.

Gender justice encompasses several principles and objectives:

- Gender Equality: Advocating for the equal rights, opportunities, and treatment of all individuals and dismantling systems perpetuating gender-based discrimination.
- Non-Discrimination: Eliminating all forms of gender-based discrimination
- Ensuring the full realization of Women's Rights
- Recognizing and supporting the rights of LGBTQIA+ individuals
- Empowerment: to exercise agency, challenging traditional gender roles and norms that limit opportunities and choices.
- Social transformation.

Economic Justice

Economic justice refers to fairness and equality in the distribution of financial resources, opportunities, and outcomes within a society, with equal access to basic needs of food, housing, healthcare, education, and employment. It recognizes that economic systems can produce disparities and inequalities, leading to social and economic injustices. Economic justice seeks to address these imbalances and create a more equitable society where everyone can prosper and lead a dignified life.

Economic justice encompasses several principles and goals:

- Redistribution of wealth more equitably, reducing extreme disparities between the rich and the poor.
- Equal opportunities by eliminating financial barriers.
- Emphasizing the need for fair work compensation and protecting workers' rights.
- Providing affordable financial services to individuals and communities historically marginalized or excluded from the mainstream financial system.
- Considering the long-term impact of economic activities on the environment and future generations.

Environmental Justice

Environmental justice refers to the fair and equitable treatment of individuals and communities when developing, implementing, and enforcing environmental policies, regulations, and practices. It recognizes that marginalized and disadvantaged communities often bear a disproportionate burden of environmental hazards and suffer from the adverse impacts of environmental degradation.

Fundamental principles and objectives of environmental justice include:

- Ensuring that no individual or community experiences a higher level of environmental harm or is denied access to environmental benefits based on race, income, or other social factors.
- Recognizing all individuals have the right to live in a clean, safe, and healthy environment and advocating for the protection of environmental quality.
- Involving affected communities in decision-making processes related to environmental policies, projects, and regulations.

- Enabling fair and transparent decision-making processes that allow meaningful participation and input from all stakeholders.
- Promoting environmentally sustainable practices that protect ecosystems, conserve natural resources, and encourage long-term well-being while ensuring that the benefits and costs of environmental decision-making are distributed equitably.

WOKE CONCEPTS

Intersectionality

Intersectionality is at the core of social justice activism. It is a concept developed by legal scholar and black feminist writer Kimberlé Crenshaw and outlined in her 1989 paper *Demarginalizing the intersection of race and sex* (Crenshaw, 1989). Intersectionality recognizes that individuals hold multiple identities and can experience various forms of oppression and discrimination based on their intersecting identities, such as race, gender, sexuality, class, and ability.

Intersectionality seeks to understand and address these entwined systems of privilege and oppression to create a more inclusive and equitable society. Wokeism addresses these issues holistically and systematically in the modern world. Crenshaw herself states, "The phrase 'stay woke' really comes out of the idea that if you don't understand how oppression works, you can't be effective in addressing it. And intersectionality really is the tool that helps us understand how oppression works."

Allyship

Allyship is a process where those who hold privilege can use their power and influence to support marginalized communities and help dismantle systems of oppression. For example, acknowledging that there is still systemic racism within America, that unconscious bias against minorities still exists, and that white people are privileged in most areas of society are essential to this principle. By challenging these unconscious biases and their sensitivity or "white fragility" around racism, white people can embrace anti-racist ideals and be allies to people of color by actively opposing racism and amplifying their voices.

Safe Spaces

Wokeism also focuses on creating safe spaces through a culture of empathy and understanding. It promotes dialogue and education around issues related to identity and marginalization, also known as "political correctness." It creates opportunities for individuals to express their experiences and perspectives. A safe space can be in the digital or physical world, encompassing psychological, emotional, and physical safety.

Decolonization

Colonialism refers to establishing and maintaining political and economic control over foreign territory and its indigenous population by a foreign power. Colonial powers typically exploit the resources and labor of the colonized region while often disregarding the rights and well-being of the indigenous population. Colonialization by the founders of America has had lasting effects on its Indigenous peoples, and decolonization is believed necessary for healing and justice (Tuck & Yang, 2012).

Hierarchy of Oppression

The hierarchy of oppression recognizes that different forms intersect and interact, creating a complex system of power dynamics and inequalities. Specific forms of oppression, such as racism, sexism, homophobia, transphobia, ableism, and classism, are deeply ingrained in society and have historically marginalized and disadvantaged certain groups. It acknowledges that the impact of oppression can vary depending on an individual's intersecting identities and the social, cultural, and economic contexts in which they exist.

This framework highlights that oppression operates on multiple levels, from individual interactions and biases to institutional policies and societal structures. By recognizing and challenging the hierarchy of oppression, social justice advocates aim to create a more inclusive and equitable society that dismantles systems of privilege and discrimination and uplifts the voices and experiences of marginalized groups.

Political Correctness

Political correctness encompasses attempts to avoid language and actions that might be considered offensive, discriminatory, or insensitive towards certain groups related to gender, race, age, ethnicity, religion, and disability. At its core, political correctness aims to promote inclusivity, respect, and sensitivity toward marginalized communities. It seeks to challenge and rectify historical prejudices, discrimination, and stereotypes.

Political Correctness is a concept inherited from the 1980s and 90s, known as "PC" language. It redefined masculine and feminine nouns into neutral nouns, which are now normalized and accepted in everyday speech. Today, the politically correct language includes the use of gender-neutral pronouns when referring to people who identify as non-binary (neither male nor female). It also includes choosing language that does not reflect oppressive relationships, such as using "master" or "inmate," or does not have derogatory gender or racial connotations.

Wokeness is often a shorthand for "political correctness"

because of concerns that language policing and censorship by woke individuals have gone too far. Some believe this can inhibit open dialogue and constructive debate on essential issues, potentially leading to self-censorship, where individuals refrain from expressing their views due to fear of backlash. As a result, "political correctness" has become a derogatory term, disapproving of those zealously over-policing and censoring free speech.

An extensive study of online communities in 2017 called *Hidden Tribes: A Study of America's Polarized Landscape* (Hawkins et al., 2018) discovered almost all Conservatives are concerned about political correctness, while fewer Liberals and Progressives see it as a problem.

It is important to note that while woke principles and concepts are intended to foster inclusivity and equality, their interpretation can be subjective and contentious. Balancing the need for respectful dialogue and protecting marginalized groups with the principles of free expression is an ongoing challenge for society.

3

"THE WOKE"

"Woke" is an adjective describing various people and their stereotyped characteristics. The more positive characterization is: a young, well-educated, progressive, anti-conservative, socially conscious and politically aware, racially diverse, self-expressed, and motivated to change oppressive and discriminative systems.

Conversely, the negative stereotypes of a "Woke" person range from the entitled Gen Z, pretentious academic, or wealthy CEO, to the radical, outspoken, anti-authoritarian, angry activist, or self-righteous, punitive, and hypocritical online social justice warrior (SJW).

These perceptions of "Woke" people are common but not necessarily accurate. The "Woke" is a diverse group that can be categorized according to demographics, beliefs, and political preferences. One-third of American voters identify as woke (Schulte, 2021), and researchers have gathered data and sorted them into several subtypes.

GEN Z: THE WOKE GENERATION

Generation Z, or Gen Z, is the demographic cohort born between the mid-to-late 1990s and the early 2010s. This generation grew up in a rapidly evolving technological and cultural landscape, and their attitudes toward social issues reflect this. Gen Z (and, to some degree, younger Millennials) is often called the "Woke Generation" due to their social and political consciousness; however, political researchers David Mclennan and Ross Whitney believe that Gen Z overall may not be as woke as people think (Mclennan & Whitney, 2022).

Social Justice Activism

According to studies on Gen Z conducted by the Pew Research Center, racial and ethnic diversity, climate change, and LGBTQIA+ rights are among the issues that Gen Z are most likely to say they care about (Geiger & Davis, 2019). This generation's social and political activism is fuelled by their exposure to progressive ideals through education and social media access, allowing them to connect with like-minded individuals and amplify their voices. This emphasis on social justice issues put Gen Z at the forefront of movements such as Black Lives Matter, Fridays for Future, and the Global Climate Strike (Alphonse, 2019).

Social Awareness

Mclennan and Whitney believe that Gen Z's attitudes to social justice issues are not just because of education and social media but due to their experiences shaped by growing up with mass school shootings, racial brutalities, and the Covid-19 pandemic. This volatile environment has made the woke generation overall more empathetic to the needs of marginalized people and more likely to support government interventions and left-leaning ideas (Mclennan & Whitney, 2022).

Progressiveness

In addition, Gen Z voters in the 18 to 29 age group are most likely to hold anti-conservative views around political correctness, CRT, affirmative action, and reverse discrimination; and more likely to drive progressiveness, according to Natalie Jackson, a researcher on social attitudes (Khazan, 2021b). A recent Meredith Poll shows that Gen Z holds some of the most liberal views and is most likely to support abortion rights, protection for LGBTQIA+ persons, and the legalization of marijuana (Mclennan & Whitney, 2022).

Illiberalism

Mclennan and Whitney also found less emphasis on democracy among Gen Z, with half believing it is more important to have a strong leader than a strong democracy, more than any other age group studied. In addition, two-thirds of Gen Z favor using force to protect the American way of life (Mclennan & Whitney, 2022). While these results may be alarming, they demonstrate a trend by Gen Z towards illiberalism and challenging systems they see as ineffective, not necessarily through a democratic process.

Racial and Gender Diversity

Despite their political leanings, Gen Z and their sub-groups are the most racially, ethnically, and gender diverse. They are the least affiliated with a religion of all age groups, and according to a 2020 Pew Research Center Survey, one-fifth of Gen Z identify as LGBTQIA+ (Jones, 2023). As a result, they are more likely to embrace non-traditional gender and sexual identities and more vocal about their support for equal rights (Parker et al., 2019).

Conservatism

The research also pointed to a deeper divide within Gen Z based on gender. Many Gen Z males hold more conservative views on the role of women and black candidates in political office, preferring white male leaders. Whereas the majority of Gen Z women feel that there are not enough females or black people in politics because they are held back by males generally (Mclennan & Whitney, 2022).

There is a common misconception that everyone under 25 is a "Progressive Woke." However, Reem Nadeem has analyzed many political typologies and, as with any generation, Gen Z has a diverse range of political alliances, with most identifying as Outsider Left (40%) and Progressive Left (34%), and fewer aligned with Faith and Flag Conservativism (8%) (Nadeem, 2021c). The large-scale study on political typology provided additional differentiation on "The Woke" based on factors other than age, such as education levels, racial diversity, wealth, and geographic location.

OUTSIDER LEFT

A higher proportion of Gen Z makes up the group defined as the Outsider Left. They are politically distinct from the Progressive Left: They are more racially diverse, less likely to have a college degree, and are from lower socio-economic backgrounds. The Outsider Left is the most disenfranchised at government ineffectiveness, showing little alignment with Liberal or Democrat politics. As a result, they have little confidence in government structures, social reforms, or progressive liberalism. They are also least engaged in partisan political debate (Nadeem, 2021d).

PROGRESSIVE LEFT

Those who identify politically as Progressive Left are most aligned with defined "woke ideologies." They are generally described as very liberal and highly educated, and the majority are white. Most of the Progressive Left (71%) are under 50, reflecting the high proportion of Gen Z, Millennial, and Gen X cohorts that make up this younger political group which is still more diverse than conservative groups. The Progressive Left has the highest share of college graduates (48%), and half are religiously affiliated (Nadeem, 2021a).

Education Levels

However, some studies support findings that being Woke is not necessarily reliant on being highly educated, with many young people becoming more progressive, even though they have not been to college yet, or will never go to college (Khazan, 2021a). Gen Z is showing up to college with progressive ideas due to their exposure in K–12 schools and the rise of platforms such as Facebook and Twitter (Khazan, 2021b). Nevertheless, the Progressive Left is the most anti-conservative political group.

Research also reinforces that the relationship between wokeness and education could be overstated. There is little difference in attitudes on "hot-topic woke issues" and people's level of education. One topic that did show a marked difference was freedom of speech. Those with college degrees are more likely to support speakers who freely express viewpoints on race or gender that some may find offensive (Khazan, 2021b).

Khazen also points out that historically, a third of all Americans (36%) have obtained a degree, and most attended state schools. As a result, many middle-aged, middle-income conservative college graduates do not identify as woke, despite a progressive liberal education.

Political Engagement

Although the Progressive Left represents one of the minority groups of registered voters (7%), they are among the most politically engaged, with the highest voting rate (86%). In addition, almost half of the Progressive Left (44%) say they follow government and public affairs most of the time and strongly align with liberals on many social issues (Nadeem, 2021a).

Belief in White Advantage

The Progressive Left supports issues such as expanding the size and scope of government, foreign policy, immigration, and race. They support the Black Lives Matter movement, addressing white advantage and other racial issues. They believe that white people benefit from social advantages not available to black people and that most US institutions need to be rebuilt because they are fundamentally biased against some races and ethnicities (Nadeem, 2021a).

Middle-Income

Most of the Progressive Left (51%) are in the middle-income bracket, with only 22% in the high-income bracket, and broadly support increasing taxes for large corporations and high-income households. Many support defunding police, and they are most critical of the US, believing other countries are better off (Nadeem, 2021a).

THE WOKE ELECT

The "Woke Elect" or "Cultural Elite" are portrayed by anti-woke authors, such as John McWhorter (McWhorter, 2021a), Vivek Ramaswamy in *Woke Inc* (Ramaswamy, 2021), and Joanne Williams in *How Woke Won* (J. Williams, 2022) as an elite group of (mostly) white, wealthy, male, well-educated Boomers and GenX CEOs, public administrators, and academics. Much of the formal woke ideology today was developed in academia by professional anthropologists, political scientists, legal analysts, psychologists, and educators. Feminist authors from the 1970s and 80s developed concepts such as Critical Race Theory, Social Theory, Gender Identity Theory, and Intersectionality that have influenced successive generations of academics, political and corporate leaders, and activists.

The Elect are both revered and blamed for the prevalence of Wokeism today. They are regarded by many critics as the invisible drivers behind progressive activism, corporate Wokeism, and many social reforms today. Although many of the Elect are aging "Boomers" and are now retired, their legacy of progressive ideology has been adopted by successive generations of liberal "Gen X" who occupy the majority of university teaching positions, corporate management, and public office today.

The Wealthy Woke

The Wealthy Woke is an influential sub-group promoting woke ideology in Corporate America. According to Ramaswamy, they are identified as predominantly white, well-educated, and wealthy. They grew up in cities and were educated in a liberal progressive school system. They have the resources and influence to shape the policies of large corporations and organizations. Although they represent only a small number of voters, their presence is felt through media advertising, the arts, film and television, sport, retail, and finance industries. The Pew Research Center results indicate that a fifth of politicians and corporate leaders are wealthy Progressives; however, there are equally as many wealthy Conservatives, so "wealth" itself is not the dominant factor for being Woke (Nadeem, 2021a).

The "Woke" consists of some of these diverse sub-types but share some common social and political beliefs and attitudes broadly defined as Wokeism or Woke Culture.

4

EVOLUTION OF WOKEISM

Wokeism is generally associated with progressive liberalism, a political ideology that emerged from classic liberalism and leftism in the late 19th century and evolved during the Progressive Era of political and social reform in the early 20th century. However, proponents of Wokeism believe it goes beyond a political ideology and describes an attitude and value system unique to these times.

Traditionally, political parties were a coalition of people who shared common industries, regional locations, or interests but were not defined by their moral or religious stance. For instance, during the Civil Rights movement and the Vietnam War, there were liberal Republicans and conservative Democrats (Pappas, 2012). However, today's politically polarized society shows a decisive Left/Right split, with the Woke being associated with the Progressive Left, which is more "left-leaning" than Liberalism.

Classic Liberalism

Liberalism has its roots in the Enlightenment era of the 18th century, which emphasized individual liberty, free markets, and equality before the law. Liberalism in the United States has traditionally been associated with the Democratic Party, characterized by a belief in the democratic power of the government to protect individual rights and provide social services.

Leftism

Leftism is a more radical political ideology rooted in socialist and Marxist theory and emphasizes the need for collective action to achieve social justice and equality. Leftism in the United States is associated with socialist and progressive movements, and many believe Leftism underpins social activism today. However, many woke people do not align with or endorse socialist or Marxist ideologies.

Libertarianism

Supporters of wokeism are often mistaken for Libertarians, who believe in individual liberty, limited government intervention, and free markets. Wokeism and Libertarianism advocate for free speech and the right to challenge the political process but diverge on critical issues of government intervention, property ownership, and the rights of individuals.

Progressive Liberalism

Progressive Liberalism is a political ideology that emerged in the United States after the Civil War and extended from the

1880s to the 1920s. It was a response to the social and economic problems that arose due to industrialization and urbanization, such as poverty, inequality, corruption, and worker exploitation. It evolved from classical liberalism but placed greater emphasis on the role of government in promoting social and economic justice (Schambra, 2023).

One of the earliest progressive movements was the Populist Party, which emerged in the 1890s. The Populists were concerned about the concentration of wealth and power in the hands of a few elites. Several presidents were instrumental in furthering Progressive Liberalism in the United States: Theodore Roosevelt, Franklin D. Roosevelt, Woodrow Wilson, Lyndon B. Johnson, and Barack Obama. They brought significant advancements and expanded government intervention in social justice, civil rights, social welfare, financial regulation, education, and healthcare reforms.

According to William Schambra, a political scientist, progressiveness has been modified over the last few decades. It has become "the predominant view in modern American education, media, popular culture, and politics today," being so pervasive it has become the "norm" and generally accepted by conservatives and liberals alike (Schambra, 2023).

Progressive Liberalism aligns with Wokeism by supporting policies and reforms to reduce inequality, promote diversity, and challenge traditional power structures. It prioritizes racial justice, LGBTQIA+ rights, gender equality, and environmental protection. Similarly, Leftism's emphasis on collective action and structural change aligns with the woke movement's focus on directly challenging systemic issues.

ACADEMIC INFLUENCE ON WOKEISM

Several academic theories were developed during the 1970s when progressives lobbied for anti-racism, anti-sexism, and anti-discrimination reforms. These theories challenged the very concepts of race, gender, and social identity. Still, their application in developing diversity and equity policies for education and workplaces has had many impacts. Although Critical Race and Social Identity Theories have underpinned social, political, and education systems for decades, they are mistakenly attributed to "Wokeism."

Critical Race Theory

Critical Race Theory (CRT) is an academic framework that emerged in the United States during the late 1970s and early 1980s. It is an interdisciplinary approach to studying race and racism that seeks to understand how racism operates in society, particularly in the law and legal system. According to CRT scholars such as Richard Delgardo and Jean Stefancic, in their 2017 book *Critical Race Theory,* racism is not just an individual problem but a systemic and institutionalized one that pervades society at all levels (Delgado & Stefancic, 2017).

While the civil rights movement had successfully challenged the most overt forms of discrimination, CRT scholars argued that racism is deeply ingrained in the structure and culture of American society. Accordingly, they sought to uncover how society perpetuates racism through seemingly neutral laws, policies, implicit biases, and cultural norms used to maintain white people's social and economic dominance. One of the earliest proponents of CRT was legal scholar Derrick Bell. Other prominent scholars include Mari Matsuda and Kimberlé Crenshaw (Delgado & Stefancic, 2017).

CRT has had a significant impact on both the political and education systems in the United States. In the education system, CRT has influenced how educators approach issues of race and racism in the classroom and should not be confused with "critical thinking," a learning process also taught in schools. Some believe CRT provides a more nuanced and accurate understanding of how racism operates and can help non-marginalized students develop greater understanding and empathy for marginalized communities. In addition, CRT encourages marginalized students to be recognized and their experiences of racism validated (West, 2021).

Gender Theory

Gender theory is a field that examines the social and cultural construction of gender, including how gender identities are created and intersect with other aspects of social identity. One way in which gender theory relates to progressive ideologies is by challenging traditional gender roles and stereotypes. Prominent feminist theorists, such as Judith Butler, argue that gender is not a fixed biological category but a fluid and socially constructed identity shaped by social norms, cultural values, and power relations (Szorenyi, 2022).

Gender theorists such as Laura Erickson-Schroth and Ben Davis, authors of *Gender: What Everyone Needs to Know* (Erickson-Schroth & Davis, 2021), take this argument further, questioning the very idea of binary gender categories (i.e., male/female) and advocating for a more expansive understanding of gender identity. They reject the idea that there are only two fixed genders and instead embrace that gender is a spectrum that includes a range of identities and expressions.

Social Identity Theory

Social Identity Theory is a related concept that explains how individuals form and maintain their sense of self according to their social group. According to social identity theory scholars Michael Kalin and Nicholas Sambanis, individuals categorize themselves and others into social groups based on shared characteristics such as gender, race, or nationality (Kalin & Sambanis, 2018). As a result, people derive their sense of self-esteem from their membership in these groups.

These ideas underpin woke ideologies seeking gender equality and LGBTQIA+ rights. For example, advocates for transgender rights argue that individuals should be able to express their gender identity freely, regardless of their biological sex or assigned gender at birth.

Similarly, advocates for gender equality seek to challenge gender stereotypes and promote gender diversity and inclusion in education, the workplace, and other areas of social life.

Critical race theory and social and gender theory are essential frameworks for challenging and dismantling systems of oppression and privilege and drive the process of social justice activism. However, critics of these theories, including many academics, have expressed concerns that their overuse and exaggerated focus on race and gender restricts free speech, creating an environment of intellectual intolerance and censorship. They say this is antithetical to the process of inquiry and constructive debate fundamental to academic discourse.

5

WOKE ACTIVISM

The academic environment has nurtured Gen Z's heightened sense of justice through teaching progressive ideology, providing a structure to think and debate about social justice issues, and empowering them to act. The woke generation has embraced the spirit of social reform inherited from the 1960s. They have reinvigorated the concept of protest: marching, boycotting, and non-violent confrontation, and adopted social media to disseminate opinions, call out offensive behaviors, and bring accountability to a perceived dysfunctional system.

Wokeism has been a unifying umbrella for various social justice issues, and activism movements flourished because of the focus on furthering social reforms. Social activism raises awareness and sparks conversations encouraging people to think critically about the world and how they can contribute to meaningful change.

Some of the benefits of social activism include:

- Encouraging inclusivity and diversity to recognize and celebrate differences to create a more tolerant and accepting society.
- Empowering marginalized communities by giving them a platform to voice their concerns and advocate for a more equitable society.
- Encouraging institutions to be accountable for promoting transparency and ethical behavior where everyone is held to the same standards.

Several social justice issues have been grouped under the banner of the "Woke Movement." Large-scale movements such as Black Lives Matter and Me Too provided a model for many other groups and brought awareness to many social justice issues.

ANTI-RACISM ACTIVISM

Anti-racism relies on the belief that racism is a pervasive and systemic issue that society must actively oppose through education, advocacy, and policy changes (Mandelaro, 2021). For example, high-profile advocates of anti-racism, such as Robyn DiAngelo, Dr. Ibram X. Kendi, and Dr. Luke Woods, stress that "not-being-racist" is no longer enough to counter systemic racism and that white people, especially, can show their support through proactive anti-racist actions (Chotiner, 2021; Mandelaro, 2021). This view is rejected by some conservative critics, who claim this is reverse racism toward white people (Linker, 2021; Lyons, 2023; Nadeem, 2021c; Rufo, 2021).

Black Lives Matter (BLM) Movement

The BLM movement has been prominent in advocating against police brutality and systemic racism against black people. It has sparked nationwide protests, policy reforms, and increased awareness of racial injustice.

Criminal Justice Reform Movement

This movement has aimed to address mass incarceration, unfair sentencing, and prisoners' treatment resulting from systemic racism. It has led to reforms in sentencing laws, increased focus on rehabilitation, and discussions about alternatives to traditional punitive measures.

Education Equity Movement

Activists have fought for equal access to quality education, particularly for disadvantaged communities. This movement has highlighted disparities in educational resources, advocated for school funding reform, and promoted initiatives to close the achievement gap.

Indigenous Rights Movement

Indigenous activists have fought for land rights, cultural preservation, and recognition of their sovereignty. These efforts have resulted in legal victories, increased awareness of historical injustices, and improved representation for indigenous peoples.

Immigration Rights Movement

Activists have called for comprehensive immigration reform, advocating for immigrants' rights and fair treatment. This movement has influenced policy debates, raised awareness about immigrant experiences, and pushed for more inclusive and compassionate immigration policies.

GENDER EQUITY ACTIVISM

This social justice issue recognizes that gender-based discrimination and violence is a global problem that affects people of all genders, and the belief that gender equity is essential for achieving social justice.

Feminist Movement

Feminist activism has sought to address gender inequality and promote gender equity in various spheres of life for many decades. It has contributed to advancements in women's rights, reproductive rights, and the dismantling of gender-based discrimination.

Me Too Movement

After gaining traction in 2017, the Me Too movement brought attention to the widespread prevalence of sexual harassment and assault against women. It encouraged survivors to share their experiences, leading to increased accountability for perpetrators and changes in workplace policies.

LGBTQIA+ Rights Movement

The LGBTQIA+ rights movement has fought for equality, marriage rights, and anti-discrimination protections. The campaign has contributed to legalizing same-sex marriage in several countries and passing laws protecting LGBTQIA+ individuals.

ENVIRONMENTAL JUSTICE ACTIVISM

Environmental Justice is based on the belief that environmental issues intertwine with social justice issues and that marginalized communities often bear the brunt of environmental degradation. The Environmental justice activism has had significant positive impacts on corporate policies and strategies.

Climate Justice Movement

This movement advocates for environmental justice and addresses the disproportionate impact of climate change on marginalized communities. It has mobilized efforts to reduce carbon emissions, promote renewable energy, and raise awareness about the need for sustainable practices.

DISABILITY RIGHTS ACTIVISM

Disability rights involve recognizing that people with disabilities have the right to inclusion in all aspects of society and the belief that "ableism" is a form of discrimination that must be challenged.

Disability Rights Movement

This movement advocates for equal rights, accessibility, and inclusion for people with disabilities. It has contributed to the passage of the Americans with Disabilities Act (ADA) and other legislation protecting the rights of individuals with disabilities.

ECONOMIC EQUALITY ACTIVISM

Wealth inequality is a major social issue contributing to other forms of inequality and the belief that economic justice is essential for social justice and reforms. For example, the Fight for $15 movement advocates for a fair living wage for all workers (Fight for $15, 2023).

ONLINE ACTIVISM

Wokeism has influenced how people engage with and discuss various topics on social media platforms (Facebook, Tik-Tok, Twitter, Instagram), which provide a way for people to connect with others who share their values and organize around social and political issues. Activists use social media platforms to organize protests, share information about social justice issues, and call out instances of discrimination or bias. Using hashtags such as #StayWoke and #MeToo has helped amplify marginalized communities' voices and draw attention to issues that might have gone unnoticed.

A 2022 Pew Research Center study on social media impacts confirms young people are more likely to use social media and to have positive opinions about it. However, the age gap has closed over the past decade with a sharp increase in social media use amongst 30 to 50-year-olds, which includes those who identify as woke (Greenwood & Wike, 2022).

Benefits of Social Media

The study revealed several positive benefits of social media on politics, views held mainly by those under 50:

- Good for democracy and politics
- Provides a sense of empowerment for everyday citizens to express their concerns and share personal experiences
- Keeping informed about domestic and international events

- More accepting of diverse cultures and different backgrounds
- An effective tool for accomplishing political goals
- Raising public awareness
- Changing people's minds about issues
- Getting elected officials to pay attention to issues
- Influencing policy decisions
- Mobilize audiences for social change
- Use calling out as a means of drawing attention to problematic behaviors
- Fostering accountability through public exposure
- Listening to and amplifying marginalized voices
- Challenge dominant narratives
- Foster inclusivity

Although a more recent Pew Research Center poll supports this claim, with most people saying social media is an effective tool for political change, far fewer people think that social media changes people's thoughts about social or political decisions or influences policy decisions (Clancy, 2023).

Criticisms of Social Media

- Call-Out Culture can fuel online harassment and hate speech
- Makes people more divisive
- People are less civil in how they talk about politics
- Uses "fake news" to spread misinformation and disinformation
- Deepened distrust between opposing political parties
- Polarizing political supporters of different parties and exacerbating political tensions
- Algorithms create echo chambers reinforcing particular views and ignoring others.

- Increased online tribalism
- Bad influence on democracy

The 2022 study indicated that most Americans (79%) believe social media has divided people in their political opinions and are less civil in discussing politics (69%). In addition, most Americans (64%) believe the internet and social media are bad for democracy, and more so in the United States than in other countries (Greenwood & Wike, 2022).

The study identified only a quarter of Americans (23%) post political messages on social media; however, conservative Republicans and liberal Democrats (not the Progressive Left) use social media the most, despite Republicans being the most concerned about its negative impacts (Clancy, 2023).

Overall, most Americans, conservative and liberal, have similar views on the limited impact of the media and its role in the "Culture War."

PERFORMATIVE ACTIVISM

While Woke activism movements have effectively promoted positive change, they are sometimes criticized for being performative. Performative activism, sometimes called "virtue signaling," describes actions or statements primarily aimed at supporting a social or political cause without actively contributing to meaningful change or addressing the root issues. Being performative is engaging in activism to appear socially conscious or progressive and is often superficial or self-serving. Typically it involves minimal personal sacrifice or discomfort, short-term engagement, and a lack of accountability (Stollznow, 2022).

Symbolic Gestures

Performative activists tend to engage in symbolic gestures with limited impact or substance. This can include sharing social justice-related posts on social media without taking any further action, wearing trendy clothing or accessories associated with a cause without engaging in deeper understanding or advocacy, or participating in a one-time event or protest without sustained commitment.

Performative activism can undermine genuine efforts toward social change by distracting attention from marginalized communities' voices and needs, perpetuating a sense of complacency, and hindering the progress of meaningful collective action.

Slactivism

"Slacktivism" or "hashtag activism" refers to supporting a social cause online through likes, shares, and hashtags without taking any meaningful action. While social media can be a powerful tool for raising awareness, critics argue that "slacktivism" can be counterproductive if it leads people to believe they've done their part by simply posting about an issue online.

Social Justice Warriors

The term "social justice warrior" (SJW) was initially used to refer to highly motivated individuals actively advocating for social justice causes, often online. The label was co-opted by performative activists more focused on optics and "virtue signaling" than meaningful change. The anti-woke use SJW as a derisive insult to suggest individuals are overly politically correct or extreme in their views.

CORPORATE ACTIVISM

Wokeism's influence on social media has extended to corporations, with many companies embracing social justice causes to align with the values of their target audience. Brands have used social media platforms to showcase their commitment to diversity, equity, and inclusion, often through statements, campaigns, or sponsorships. However, this trend has also been criticized as performative activism or "woke-washing" when not accompanied by substantial systemic change (Spry et al., 2022).

Many companies have embraced progressive marketing strategies in their advertising to promote messages of diversity and inclusivity. For example, media campaigns have featured people of color, LGBTQIA+ individuals, and people with disabilities in ads promoting social justice issues such as racial equality and gender equity (Willis, 2022).

SPORTS ACTIVISM

Wokeism has notably impacted sports recently, with athletes, leagues, and organizations becoming more vocal and engaged in social and political agendas.

Athlete Activism

Wokeism has empowered athletes to use their platform to speak out and advocate for social justice causes. Notable examples include Colin Kaepernick, who started the "Take a Knee" protest during the national anthem in the NFL to raise awareness about police brutality and racial injustice (Haislop, 2020). LeBron James, one of the most influential basketball players, has been vocal about racial equality, addressing issues such as police brutality and founding the "More Than A Vote" organization to combat voter suppression (The Athletic, 2021).

Corporate Sponsorship

The influence of Wokeism can also be seen in corporate sponsorship decisions. Companies are increasingly aligning themselves with social justice causes and supporting athlete advocates. For example, Target announced a $10 million commitment to supporting partners like the National Urban League and the African American Leadership Forum (Target, 2020); Walmart announced that it will contribute $100 million over five years to create a new center for racial equity (Walmart, 2021). Home Depot announced a $1 million donation to the Lawyers' Committee for Civil Rights Under Law (Livingstone, 2020).

League Initiatives

Professional sports leagues have also taken steps to support social justice causes and address systemic inequalities. For instance, the National Basketball Association (NBA) launched the NBA Foundation with a $300 million commitment to support economic empowerment in black communities (Prest, 2020). In addition, the National Football League (NFL) established a social justice initiative, committing $250 million over a 10-year period to combat racial inequality (NFL, 2022).

Team and Player Protests

Wokeism is associated with increased team and player protests during games. In 2020, following the murder of George Floyd, numerous sports teams across various leagues, including the NBA, MLB, and MLS, boycotted games to raise awareness of ongoing racial injustice (Hill, 2021).

Policy Changes

Sports organizations have made policy changes to support diversity and inclusion. In 2022 Team USA announced a new strategy for diversity and inclusion for racial and social justice (Team USA, 2022). However, recent backlash against the inclusion of transgender athletes in sports has prompted a review of National Collegiate Athletics Association (NCAA) policy, and other sports codes, resulting in uncertainty for many transgender athletes (Mosier, 2022).

Although proponents applaud the increased focus on social justice, critics argue that it has politicized sports and created fan divisions.

WOKE MOVEMENTS

Social Justice activism has led to several woke movements in the last decade that have been instrumental in progressing social reforms in many countries worldwide. Most of these have originated in the United States, advanced social justice concepts, and provided a powerful means for people to participate in social change. Some high-profile social justice movements to explore in greater depth are the Black Lives Matter Movement, the Me Too Movement, the LGBTQIA+ Rights Movement, and the Climate Justice Movement.

6

THE BLACK LIVES MATTER MOVEMENT

Black Activism in the 21st century gained powerful momentum following several police brutality incidents. The tipping point was the killing of Trayvon Martin, an unarmed black teenager, in Sanford, Florida 2012. The subsequent acquittal of George Zimmerman, the neighborhood watch volunteer who shot Martin, sparked outrage and galvanized a new generation of black activists. Protests erupted nationwide, as many believed the shooting was racially motivated.

According to the Black Lives Matter website, the movement was founded in 2013 by Alicia Garza, Patrisse Cullors, and Opal Tometi and began as a hashtag on social media, #BlackLivesMatter, and has since evolved into a global movement advocating for the rights and dignity of black people. Its mission is to "eradicate white supremacy and build local power to intervene in violence inflicted on black communities by the state and vigilantes (BLM, 2019)."

The BLM movement escalated after the killing of Michael Brown, an unarmed black teenager, by a white police officer in Ferguson, Missouri, in 2014. The shooting triggered weeks of protests and civil unrest in Ferguson and other cities across the

United States. The subsequent backlash over the trial ignited a more politically charged call to action with the hashtag #StayWoke prominent amongst online black communities. This revitalized using the term in this highly charged political context (Grant, 2022).

The movement reached its height after the brutal murder of George Floyd, an unarmed black man, by a white police officer in Minneapolis, Minnesota, in May 2020. The video footage of Floyd's death, which showed the officer kneeling on Floyd's neck for more than nine minutes as he protested, "I can't breathe," sparked further outrage, a powerful slogan, and protests championing the movement globally. According to Amnesty International, it inspired 16 million people to join the protests nationwide, primarily organized and led by young people. These were some of the most extensive and sustained in American history, marking a significant turning point in the fight for racial justice (Amnesty, 2020).

HISTORY OF BLACK ACTIVISM

Black activism has a rich and diverse history in the United States. It spans several centuries, with roots dating back to the early days of slavery. It encompasses various movements, organizations, and individuals who fought against racial injustice, segregation, and discrimination. It has sought to secure civil rights, equality, and social change.

There have been three distinct waves of anti-racist activism: the Slavery Abolition Movement, the Civil Rights Movement, and, more recently, the Black Lives Matter (BLM) movement.

Abolitionist Movement

Black activism in the United States has its roots in the struggle against slavery. Enslaved Africans and African Americans, along with White abolitionists, fought for the abolition of slavery throughout the 18th and 19th centuries. Activists like Frederick Douglass, Harriet Tubman, Sojourner Truth, and David Walker played significant roles in raising awareness about the cruelty and immorality of slavery (Britannica, 2023).

Civil Rights Movement

The Civil Rights Movement was a pivotal era of black social activism. Led by figures such as Martin Luther King Jr., Rosa Parks, Malcolm X, and many others, the movement aimed to end racial segregation and secure equal rights under the law. It included significant events like the Montgomery Bus Boycott, the March on Washington, the Selma to Montgomery marches, and the passage of landmark legislation like the *Civil Rights Act of 1964* and the *Voting Rights Act of 1965* (US House of Representatives, 2023).

Black Power Movement

Emerging in the late 1960s and early 1970s, the Black Power Movement sought to empower Black communities, challenge systemic racism, and promote self-determination. Influential organizations such as the Black Panther Party and figures like Stokely Carmichael (later known as Kwame Ture) emphasized self-defense, Black pride, and political and economic empowerment (NMAAHC, 2021; Webster, 2022).

BLM MOVEMENT IN ACTION

The BLM movement has used various tactics to raise awareness of police brutality and criminal justice; these include protests, civil disobedience, and social media campaigns. However, the most significant impact has been its focus on policing and criminal justice, leading to increased scrutiny and reform efforts. In addition, a wide range of activists, celebrities, and politicians, have used their public platforms to amplify the message of the BLM movement beyond the issue of police brutality, raising awareness of systemic racism.

According to a 2020 Pew Research Center survey on public attitudes to the BLM movement, most Americans (67%) support the BLM movement and black activism, with the most prominent supporters being Black, young, Gen Z, and Millennials (Horowitz et al., 2023).

Awareness of racism

The BLM movement has brought systemic racism to the forefront of public consciousness, which extends beyond policing to include housing, education, and employment issues. The 2020 survey showed most Americans (71%) believe that racial discrimination is still a big problem in the US and has increased since 2016. A third of Americans (32%), particularly younger generations (49%), say the BLM Movement has effectively brought attention to racism against black people (Horowitz et al., 2023).

Corporate social responsibility

The BLM movement has also influenced corporations' response to racial justice issues. Many companies have made public statements supporting the movement and have committed to taking concrete actions to address racial inequality in their organizations. For example, in June 2020, Netflix announced it would donate $120 million to organizations supporting Black communities (Spangler, 2023), while Starbucks pledged $5 million to (Black, Indigenous, and People of Color (BIPOC) youth groups (Starbucks, 2021).

Political Influence

The movement has also impacted political discourse, with many politicians incorporating racial justice issues into their platforms. For example, during the 2020 Democratic primaries, some candidates discussed reparations for slavery and criminal justice reform (Stein, 2019). Similarly, racial justice issues played a significant role during the general election, with many voters citing it as a critical factor in their decision-making process (Nadeem, 2021b).

Cultural Activism

Black activism has also involved art, literature, music, and cultural expression. Artists like Langston Hughes, Nina Simone, Maya Angelou, and countless others have used their creative platforms to raise awareness, inspire change, and give voice to the Black experience. The BLM Movement has also impacted how Black people are portrayed in media and culture, with more attention given to black voices and perspectives.

CRITICISMS OF BLM

Lack of Meaningful Change

Despite the many positive impacts on society, a 2023 report on attitudes towards the BLM found that most Conservatives oppose the Black Lives Matter movement (Horowitz et al., 2023). One of the reasons was that although there was an increased focus on issues of race and racial inequality in the past three years, it had not resulted in meaningful change or improved the lives of black people. Most Americans still believe "black people are treated less fairly when applying for a loan or mortgage, in hiring, pay, and promotions, when seeking medical treatment, in stores or restaurants, and when voting in elections" (Horowitz et al., 2023).

Criticism is also split along racial lines, with white people more likely to describe the movement as divisive and dangerous than other racial and ethnic groups, which mostly describe it as empowering (Horowitz et al., 2023).

Anti-police Sentiment

There are concerns that the BLM movement promotes anti-police sentiment, with calls to "defund the police," which could lead to increased tension between law enforcement and the communities they serve. The research shows two-thirds of Americans say black people are still treated less fairly than white people in dealing with the police, with a smaller proportion (14%) believing that the BLM movement has increased police accountability (Horowitz et al., 2023). In addition, there have been concerns about the movement inciting violence, particularly during protests and demonstrations.

Lack of Clarity

Only a third of Americans (31%) say they understand the goals of the BLM Movement, confirming criticism that it lacks clarity in its goals and strategies. Its messaging and demands can be vague and unfocused, which could limit its effectiveness (Horowitz et al., 2023).

Overall, the rise of black activism and the BLM movement represent a powerful challenge to systemic racism in the United States. But, while progress occurs in some areas, it hasn't in others. Hence, the fight for racial justice continues.

7

ME TOO MOVEMENT

The Me Too Movement is a feminist social, political, and cultural movement that challenges gender-based inequalities and advocates for women's rights. The movement originated in the United States in 2006 but gained widespread attention in October 2017 when actress Alyssa Milano tweeted, "If you've been sexually harassed or assaulted write 'me too' as a reply to this tweet." This tweet went viral, and millions of women (and some men) shared their stories of sexual harassment and assault using the hashtag #MeToo on social media platforms, where 4.7 million users shared their stories in fewer than 24 hours (Gordon, 2022).

Initially, this phase of the Me Too movement was a response to the revelations of sexual abuse by movie producer Harvey Weinstein and the subsequent "Weinstein effect," which led to a flood of allegations against powerful men in various industries. The campaign brought attention to the prevalence of various forms of sexual abuse in workplaces. It also increased accountability for perpetrators and changes in workplace policies to prevent and address sexual misconduct (MTM, 2023).

Tarana Burke, an advocate for women based in New York,

first coined "Me Too" in 2006 when she founded the Me Too Movement (MTM, 2023). She aimed to empower women, especially those who have endured sexual violence. However, she noticed that most women don't report these cases. Considerable stigma and silence still surround this issue, and women need to know they aren't alone because others have gone through similar experiences (Brockes, 2018). The Me Too Movement began as a way for survivors of sexual harassment and sexual assault to air their grievances, share their stories, and find support. This has opened the space for many sweeping changes on both a social and legal level.

INTERSECTIONALITY AND FEMINISM

The theme of intersectionality is central to the feminist platform, which has worked for decades to address the unique experiences of women as a marginalized group. This particularly applies to black women or women of color who experience many intersecting forms of discrimination at a systemic level relating to gender, race, education, employment, and economic disparity.

A BRIEF HISTORY OF FEMINISM

First-Wave feminism

The first wave of feminism began in the late 19th century. It continued through the early 20th century, focused on securing women's right to vote, education, and employment opportunities. The first organized movement for women's rights in the US started in July 1848 with *The Declaration of Sentiments*. This affirmed women's equality with men and passed resolutions that called for the implementation of various rights, including the right to vote (Pruitt, 2022).

The modern feminist movement began with feminists like Rose Schneiderman fighting for workplace rights in the 1900s (Dreier, 2018). It continued with the suffrage movement, led by Susan B. Anthony and Elizabeth Cady Stanton. It resulted in the *19th Amendment of the American Constitution,* which ratified the right for white women to vote (Delao, 2021). However, black women and other women of color could only vote after the *Voting Rights Act* was enacted in 1965 (Grady, 2018).

Second-Wave Feminism

Second-wave feminism emerged in the 1960s and 1970s and had the explicit goal of reevaluating traditional gender roles and ending existing discrimination. It focused on various issues, including reproductive rights, workplace discrimination, and domestic violence (Grady, 2018).

Betty Friedan is credited for laying the groundwork for the second wave of feminism in 1963, and subsequently, the movement consolidated with the formation of feminist groups, such as the National Organization for Women, and the emergence of feminist literature. Betty Friedan, Gloria Steinem, and Bella Abzug established the National Women's Political Caucus to increase women's participation in the political process and promote feminist ideals in public policy (NWPC, 2023).

The achievements of second-wave feminism include:

- The Equal Pay Act's ratification and the Supreme Court's landmark decision to uphold women's reproductive freedom.
- In the landmark case Griswold v. Connecticut 1965, the Supreme Court struck down a Connecticut state law prohibiting contraceptives and establishing a legal precedent for reproductive rights and autonomy.

- Roe v. Wade, another landmark US Supreme Court case in 1973, upheld the Constitution that protects a woman's right to choose to have an abortion. A decision that in 2021 was controversially reversed (Housman, 2022).

Like the suffrage movement, critics attacked second-wave feminism for centering privileged white women in the campaign. As a result, Black women formed their own feminist organizations, like the National Black Feminist Organization (NBFO), in the early '70s (Pruitt, 2022).

Third-Wave Feminism

The third wave of feminism emerged in the 1990s, inspired by the high-profile Anita Hill case and her testimony on sexual harassment by supreme court nominee Clarence Thomas (Pruitt, 2022). It continued through the early 2000s and focused on the issues of intersectionality, body image, and sexuality. The movement included a greater diversity of voices and perspectives, including women of color, lesbians, and transgender women. 1992 was also dubbed the "Year of the Woman," and an unprecedented number of women were elected to Congress (Grady, 2018).

Black women activists were crucial in advocating for racial and gender equality: Rebecca Walker, Angela Davis, bell hooks, Audre Lorde, and Kimberlé Crenshaw. It was black feminists who highlighted how the intersectionality of race, gender, and class impacts women's experience in society and prompted the challenge to racial and patriarchal systems of oppression (Pruitt, 2022).

Fourth-Wave Feminism

Fourth-wave feminism emerged in the mid-2010s and is ongoing. It focuses on online harassment, rape culture, and gender-based violence. Social media and the internet have fuelled the movement, which has allowed for greater visibility and amplification of feminist voices.

Journalist Kristen Sollee explains that fourth-wave feminism is difficult to define. However, she identifies six characteristics: queer, sex-positive, trans-inclusive, anti-misandrist (not discriminating against men), body-positive, and digitally driven (Sollee, 2015). Online platforms have expanded the reach of fourth-wave feminism as the main spaces for debate around activism. Although, the annual Women's March, which started in 2017 after the Trump election, still utilizes traditional "feet-on-the-ground" protest strategies to show female solidarity (Women's March, 2022).

Gender-based Violence

Advocating against gender-based violence has been a fundamental goal of feminist movements. Fourth-wave Feminism is also concerned with the normalization that perpetuates 'rape culture' where sexual violence is accepted as the norm. It is also reinforced by misogynistic language and objectifying women's bodies (Broderick et al., 2014).

Greater Representation in Politics

Fourth-wave feminism continues to advocate for the representation of women in politics. In a 2020 interview with Glamour magazine, NWPC President Donna Lent stated that the organization's mission is "to increase the number of women in elected and appointed office." The importance of intersectionality is emphasized in NWPC's work, including the representation of women of color, LGBTQIA+ women, and disabled women (NWPC, 2023).

Feminist Movements

The MeToo and Times Up movements have their roots in fourth-wave feminism. Bringing dignity back to a woman's body and her right to choose what *she* wants to do with it. Women from all walks of life have begun to speak out in unison against misogyny, toxic masculinity, and patriarchal modes of thinking.

ME TOO MOVEMENT IN ACTION

Awareness of Sexual Harassment and Assault

The Me Too movement, aimed at raising awareness about sexual harassment and assault, has sparked a much-needed conversation. One of the most significant impacts has been its ability to empower women to speak out against their abusers and to demand accountability and justice. This has resulted in several states extending the statute of limitations for sexual assault cases, making it easier for survivors to seek redress (Jerkins, 2019).

National and State Legislation to Reduce Workplace Harassment

The Me Too Movement resulted in the enactment of federal and state laws designed to increase transparency, which include banning employers from enforcing arbitration agreements that require pre-dispute settlements and prohibiting confidentiality and non-disparagement clauses in some cases (Cone et al., 2022; NWLC, 2022).

President Joe Biden's *Ending Forced Arbitration of Sexual Assault and Sexual Harassment Act of 2021* significantly differentiates sexual harassment claims from other workplace discrimination and misconduct. In addition, the US Senate passed the *SPEAK Out Act*. New York became the first state to enact these laws in 2019, and since then, 15 other states have followed (Cone et al., 2022; NWLC, 2022).

Anti-harassment Policies

In addition, many companies have reevaluated their policies and procedures related to sexual harassment and assault and have implemented new measures to prevent such incidents from occurring in the workplace. This includes training employees, creating anonymous reporting channels, and holding perpetrators accountable for their behavior (Cone et al., 2022).

Creating Safer Spaces

Another impact of the MeToo movement is creating a safer environment for women by clarifying that such behavior will not be tolerated. This was demonstrated when high-profile abusers, such as Harvey Weinstein, Geoffry Epstein, and Bill Cosby, were held accountable, with some losing their jobs or being prosecuted for their behaviors. The movement has also impacted the reporting of sexual abuse against males, and LBGTQIA+ people, with victims speaking out against their abusers.

Supporting Survivors

Finally, the MeToo movement has highlighted the importance of supporting survivors of sexual harassment and assault. The MeToo.org website provides resources, counseling, and legal assistance and creates a supportive community where they can feel safe and heard (MTM, 2023). These measures have led to a significant increase in reported cases and greater awareness of the prevalence of sexual harassment and assault.

As stated by Tarana Burke, "The most powerful thing about #MeToo is the survivor sitting at home saying, 'I see myself in this movement. I am not alone.'"

CRITICISMS OF THE ME TOO MOVEMENT

False Allegations

Some people have raised concerns that the MeToo movement may lead to false allegations and damage to reputations and careers. While false allegations are rare, they can have severe consequences if innocent people are accused (Borysenko, 2020).

Stigmatizing Men

The Me Too movement has significantly impacted the entertainment and media industries, more than others, in stigmatizing men. Some men have reported feeling hesitant to interact with female colleagues for fear of being accused of misconduct. However, this impact is minimized in industries that are more male-dominated or have weaker labor protections (Bower, 2019).

Since the Me Too movement has spread globally, it has significantly changed workplace policies and public attitudes toward sexual harassment and assault. However, The data suggest that many women (62%) experience workplace harassment and almost a third do not report the incidents, even 5 years after #MeToo (Cone et al., 2022). Some critics have argued that governments and workplaces have still not done enough to address the underlying cultural and systemic issues that enable such behavior.

8

THE LGBTQIA+ MOVEMENT

The LGBTQIA+ movement is a social and political movement that advocates for the rights and acceptance of lesbian, gay, bisexual, transgender, queer, and intersex individuals. The movement has a long history, dating back to the mid-20th century Human Rights Campaign, which has achieved significant progress regarding legal recognition, visibility, and social acceptance of LGBTQIA+ individuals (GLAAD, 2023; Human Rights Campaign, 2023).

Wokeism has also highlighted how systemic inequalities and power imbalances have historically marginalized the LGBTQIA+ community and emphasized the intersectionality of LGBTQIA+ identities with other aspects of social identity, such as race and class.

WHAT DOES LGBTQIA+ MEAN?

Before exploring the LGBTQIA+ Movement, it's essential to clarify what LGBTQIA+ means. LGBTQIA+ is an evolving acronym, and the choice of which acronym to use can vary based on personal preference, cultural context, and the specific needs of a given community (The Center, 2023).

What Does Each Letter Mean?

L (Lesbian): A woman or a female-presenting person who is *only* attracted to people of the same gender.
G (Gay): Refers to a man or male-presenting person who is *only* attracted to people of the same gender.
B (Bisexual): Refers to someone whose sexual orientation includes romantic and sexual attraction to people of both one's own gender and other genders.
T (Transgender): This doesn't have much to do with sexual orientation but with how people feel about themselves and which gender they identify with. Being transgender means a person's gender identity differs from those assigned at birth.
Q (Queer or Questioning): This is a term for non-cisgender or homosexual. However, note that the word 'queer' can also be a slur, so it should only refer to someone who identifies with the term explicitly. 'Questioning' means a person is unsure of their sexual orientation or gender identity.
I (Intersex): Describes anyone born with various physical characteristics (especially concerning sex) that do not fit traditional binary definitions of male or female bodies, including hermaphroditic traits.
A (Asexual): People who do not have a sexual attraction to others.
+ (Plus): The 'plus' represents all the other gender identities and sexual orientations that don't form part of the first six letters. An example is Two-Spirit, a pan-Indigenous American identity (Cherry, 2022).

Other terms that are useful to know:

Cisgender: means their identity aligns with the gender assigned to them as infants. So, for example, if you're CisHet, you're a heterosexual male or female who identifies with the gender assigned to you.

Gender nonconforming: This term represents anyone whose gender identity or expression does not conform to the traditional masculine or feminine norms.

Gender identity: A person's internal sense of gender. They could identify as being a woman, a man, or non-binary. Consider that a person's gender identity does not necessarily correlate with the gender assigned to them at birth or how they present themselves to others.

Non-Binary: relating to or being a person who identifies with or expresses a gender identity that is neither entirely male nor entirely female.

THE LGBTQIA+ COMMUNITY

According to a 2022 Gallop survey of 10,000 people, the number of Americans identifying as LGBTQIA+ has doubled over the last decade and now comprises 7.2% of the total adults. More than half of those who identify as LGBTQIA+ also identify as bisexual, with one in five of that group saying they are gay, one in seven are lesbian, and one in ten identify as being transgender (Jones, 2023).

The survey also identified that Gen Z was the most likely subgroup to say they are LGBTQIA+ (20%), with Millennials the next highest age group (11%) compared to older generations (3%) (Jones, 2023).

Early Advocacy for Homosexuals

The movement's roots trace back to the late 19th and early 20th centuries when individuals such as Karl Heinrich Ulrichs and Magnus Hirschfeld began advocating for the rights of homosexuals. In the United States, the Mattachine Society and the Daughters of Bilitis were among the first LGBTQIA+ organizations formed in the 1950s and 1960s (Morris, 2009).

The Stonewall Riots

One of the critical milestones in the LGBTQIA+ movement was the Stonewall Riots, which took place in New York City in 1969. A police raid on the Stonewall Inn, a gay bar in Greenwich Village, led to protests and clashes between police and LGBTQIA+ activists. The riots are widely regarded as a turning point in the movement and helped to catalyze a broader push for LGBTQIA+ rights and visibility (Morris, 2009).

LGBTQIA+ Representation in Public Office

According to the Milk Foundation website, Harvey Milk was the first openly gay elected official in the United States, serving as a San Francisco Board of Supervisors member in the late 1970s. Milk was a vocal advocate for LGBTQIA+ rights and worked to pass anti-discrimination legislation in San Francisco. Unfortunately, he was assassinated in 1978, but his legacy has inspired many others to continue gender rights advocacy (Milk Foundation, 2023).

AIDS Activism

The AIDS crisis dominated the 1980s and 1990s, disproportionately affecting the LGBTQIA+ community. The crisis led to a wave of activism and advocacy, with groups such as ACT UP and the Gay Men's Health Crisis working to raise awareness and demand action from governments and healthcare providers. The crisis also spurred advances in medical research and treatment for HIV/AIDS (Morris, 2009).

Recognition and Acceptance

The LGBTQIA+ movement has also undergone significant shifts in its goals and strategies. In the movement's early days, activists focused primarily on securing legal and political rights and protections for LGBTQIA+ individuals. In recent years, the movement has shifted towards broader goals of social acceptance, cultural change, and intersectionality, recognizing how LGBTQIA+ identities intersect with other aspects of social identity, such as race, class, and ability (GLAAD, 2023).

LGBTQIA+ MOVEMENT IN ACTION

The LGBTQIA+ movement has brought attention to many issues faced by the LGBTQIA+ community and advocated for greater legal protections and rights. One of the most significant achievements has been the increased acceptance and visibility of LGBTQIA+ individuals.

Some other examples that demonstrate positive impacts:

- The portrayal of LGBTQIA+ characters in the arts, with television shows such as “Pose" and “Queer Eye,” and movies like "Moonlight," help increase acceptance and understanding of LGBTQIA+ individuals.

- Public awareness campaigns like the "It Gets Better" project have helped to reduce discrimination against LGBTQIA+ youth and promote acceptance.
- Establishing LGBTQIA+ community centers and organizations, such as The Trevor Project, which provide support and resources to LGBTQIA+ individuals and their families.
- Introducing non-binary gender options on government documents, such as passports and driver's licenses.
- The repeal of "Don't Ask, Don't Tell" in the United States military allowed LGBTQIA+ individuals to serve openly without fear of discharge.
- The removal of "Homosexuality" from the Diagnostic and Statistical Manual of Mental Disorders (DSM) in 1973.

Legalizing Same-sex Marriage

One of the LGBTQIA+ movement's most significant achievements was legalizing same-sex marriage in the United States. The landmark Supreme Court case Obergefell v. Hodges in 2015 was seen as an important milestone and a sign of increasing acceptance and inclusion of LGBTQIA+ individuals in society (Morris, 2009).

THE BACKLASH AGAINST THE LGBTQIA+ MOVEMENT

While the LGBTQIA+ movement has advocated for protections against discrimination in housing, healthcare, employment, and other areas of life, there has also been a severe backlash against LGBTQIA+ individuals and the movement itself. This has taken many forms, including hate crimes, discrimination, and the passage of anti-LGBTQIA+ laws, which can threaten the safety and well-being of LGBTQIA+ individuals (Choi, 2023; Luk, 2021).

Perpetuation of Harmful Stereotypes

Another negative impact involves perpetuating harmful stereotypes of LGBTQIA+ individuals, such as the "flamboyant gay man" or the "man-hating lesbian," which can lead to discrimination and prejudice. Additionally, certain groups within the LGBTQIA+ community have often been excluded or marginalized within the broader movement, which can lead to feelings of isolation and erasure (Runnels, 2018).

Threatening Traditional Gender Roles

With the increased use of online meeting platforms and the use of digital name tags, there has been growing use of personal pronouns such as “she/her,” “he/him,” and “they/them” to show respect for the diversity of gender identity. However, using personal pronouns has also become controversial, particularly among anti-woke groups who see this practice as threatening traditional gender roles and social order. Journalist Andrew Doyle explores the negative aspects of personal pronoun use in his 2022 *Unherd* article, with some conservatives concerned that using personal pronouns is a form of "linguistic authoritarianism" that seeks to police language and suppress dissenting opinions (Barrett, 2021; Doyle, 2022).

The LGBTQIA+ movement has evolved from activism and protest to a broader push for social acceptance and intersectional advocacy. Yet, while significant progress has occurred in recent decades, challenges remain, particularly in areas such as employment discrimination, healthcare access, and hate crime.

9

THE CLIMATE JUSTICE MOVEMENT

Wokeism is closely aligned with the Climate Justice Movement and is one of Gen Z's highest social justice priorities today (Khazan, 2021b). Climate Justice evolved out of the Green Movement of the mid-20th century and is one of many environmental issues facing Americans today. This movement addresses the intersectional impacts of climate change on marginalized communities and advocates for systemic change at local and global levels. Penn State meteorologist Gregory Jenkins says that racism is "inexorably" linked to climate change because it influences the processes that create environmental impacts and who suffer most (Kaplan, 2020).

ORIGINS OF THE ENVIRONMENTAL JUSTICE MOVEMENT

The history of environmental movements traces back to the late 19th century when John Muir, an early naturalist and conservationist, lobbied to protect national parks. He passionately advocated preserving America's natural landscapes from commercial development and exploitation (NPS, 2023).

At the same time, strenuous efforts were also being made across the US to protect the diminishing population of American bison. These groups focused on preserving wilderness areas and safeguarding wildlife from human exploitation, which resulted in President Woodrow Wilson establishing the National Park Service in 1916 (NPS, 2023).

The Green Movement

The Green Movement emerged in the 1960s and 1970s as a response to the environmental degradation caused by technology and industrialization. The movement advocated for environmental conservation, sustainability, and renewable energy, among other goals (PBS, 2014). The book "Silent Spring," written in 1962 by American biologist Rachel Carson, was instrumental in exposing pesticides' harmful and dangerous effects on humans and other animals. With the subsequent creation of the Environmental Protection Agency, DDT (a colorless, tasteless, and almost odorless pesticide) was formally banned from use in agriculture in 1972 (PBS, 2014).

The Anti-nuclear Movement

Several high-profile anti-nuclear organizations emerged during the 1970s, including Greenpeace and Friends of the Earth, who were engaged in grassroots activism to raise awareness about the risks associated with nuclear power and weapons (Greenpeace, 2022).

Global Environmental Initiatives

The Green Movement has provided a wide-ranging legacy of societal change and brought awareness to global concerns around climate change. These have been instrumental in creating international agreements such as the Montreal and Kyoto Protocols, which were negotiated in the 1980s to address ozone depletion and greenhouse gas emissions (Sunstein, 2007). Similarly, the emergence of conservation biology and ecosystem-based management in the 1990s and 2000s reflected growing concerns about ecosystem degradation.

Renewable Energy Sources

These initiatives have led to the worldwide adoption of renewable energy sources like solar and wind power that emit fewer greenhouse gases and are less environmentally harmful than fossil fuels. Surveys show most Americans support these initiatives, with a majority (69%) in favor of becoming carbon-neutral by 2050 and prioritizing the development of renewable energy sources, like wind and solar, over and above the production of fossil fuels. However, Americans are generally reluctant to phase out fossil fuels altogether, with most preferring a mix of renewables and fossil fuel sources (Tyson, 2023).

Addressing Social and Economic Inequality

While the Green movement focused on addressing environmental degradation caused by industrial and technological progress, activists began recognizing social and economic inequalities exacerbated these impacts and reinforced systems of oppression. The Green Movement was criticized for neglecting the needs and concerns of marginalized communities impacted by pollution and other environmental hazards (Kaplan, 2020).

RISE OF THE ENVIRONMENTAL JUSTICE MOVEMENT

The Environmental Justice movement began to gain momentum in the United States during the 1980s, as communities of color and low-income communities raised concerns about the disproportionate impact of environmental hazards on their neighborhoods. The movement addressed the unequal distribution of environmental burdens and benefits based on race, ethnicity, income, and other factors in alignment with the progressive ideologies of the time. For example, black and Hispanic communities were more likely to be impacted by the air pollution created by white people driving and using electricity than their own actions (Bullard Centre, 2023).

The movement for climate justice builds on the legacy of the green movement by expanding its focus to include social justice and equity concerns. It emphasizes how marginalized communities are disproportionately affected by extreme weather events and food shortages. For example, research demonstrates that climate change will cause more harm to poorer communities that are mainly home to people of color. Sarah Kaplan, a climate reporter for *The Washington Post*, describes how areas on the coast and in the South, where there is a higher proportion of BIPOC communities, are most likely to be affected by rising sea levels and the impacts of hurricanes (Kaplan, 2020).

ENVIRONMENTAL JUSTICE MOVEMENTS IN ACTION

Building Alliances

Today, the green movement encompasses various organizations and approaches to environmental activism, from advocacy and policy work to on-the-ground conservation and restoration projects. By building alliances with other social justice movements and advocating for solutions that address the needs of marginalized communities, the climate justice movement has become a powerful force for systemic change that aligns with Wokeism.

Climate Lawsuits

In recent years, climate justice groups such as Friends of the Earth International have filed many international lawsuits against various companies, alleging that they knowingly contributed to climate change and have caused harm to communities (FOEI, 2023).

Worker Transition Support

"Just Transition" campaigns such as those led by the Climate Justice Alliance ensure workers and communities affected by the transition away from fossil fuels are not left behind. These campaigns focus on supporting workers in the fossil fuel industry and promoting renewable energy development in communities impacted by pollution and environmental degradation (Climate Justice Alliance, 2023).

Indigenous-led Resistance

Several recent examples of successful environmental justice movements were led by Indigenous people and organizations such as the National Resources Defense Council (NRDC). Examples include resistance movements preventing uranium mining on Navajo and Hopi lands, the Dakota Access Pipeline dispute on the Standing Rock Indian Reservation, environmental cleanup efforts in Alaska, protecting clean water, and protecting wilderness areas and biodiversity (Jarratt-Snider & Nielsen, 2020; NRDC, 2023).

Community-led Energy Solutions

The Be Initiative supports Community-led energy solutions such as solar projects and energy cooperatives, which have recently gained popularity, benefitting historically underserved communities (Ayala, 2021; BE Initiative, 2023).

YOUTH-LED CLIMATE ACTIVISM

Environmental activism has historically been driven by white men. However, a new generation of young advocates, the woke generation, has taken up the challenge and spearheads America's youth climate movement. With more diversity encouraged in education systems, a 2019 poll found that there are at least twice as many black and Hispanic teens than white teens engaged in school protests and walkouts, bringing a new level of moral outrage to the issues of environmental justice (Nadeem & Tyson, 2021). Young people are more aware of the disproportionate impacts of natural disasters and more committed to taking prompt action (Kaplan, 2020).

Sunrise Movement

One of the most well-known climate justice movements is the Sunrise Movement. The movement was founded in 2017 by a group of young people responding to political leaders' lack of action on climate change. The group has organized several high-profile protests and activities, including a sit-in at Nancy Pelosi's office in November 2018 and a rally outside the Democratic National Committee headquarters in June 2019 (Sunrise Movement, 2023).

The Sunrise Movement has raised awareness about the urgent need for action on climate change, which has helped push the issue higher up on the political agenda. As a result, the

Green New Deal resolution was introduced in Congress in 2019 with the support of many climate justice advocates (Sunrise Movement, 2023).

Zero Hour Movement

The Zero Hour movement was founded by a group of young women of color, which seeks to center the voices of marginalized communities in the fight against climate change (Zero Hour, 2023).

Youth Climate Strikes

The Fridays for Future movement, inspired by a Swedish teenager, Greta Thunberg, involves young people worldwide striking from school to demand action on climate change (Fridays For Future, 2021; Henley, 2023).

The Youth Climate Strikes have drawn attention to the urgent need for climate action, particularly by young people who will bear the brunt of the impacts of climate change. The strikes have also successfully pressured governments to act on climate change. For example, in March 2019, more than 1.4 million young people in over 100 countries participated in a Youth Climate Strike, increasing media coverage and political attention (Fridays For Future, 2021).

Unintended Consequences of the Green Movement

Some actions taken in the name of the Green movement have had unintended consequences. For example, the widespread adoption of biofuels has led to deforestation and habitat loss in some regions. In addition, some large-scale renewable energy projects, such as wind and solar farms, have been criticized for impacting wildlife and local ecosystems (Vaughan, 2010).

Another issue with the green movement is the uneven distribution of its benefits. For example, these environmental actions may disproportionately affect low-income communities and communities of color, adversely impacted by renewable energy sources' location and construction process (UCSUSA, 2023).

Youth Climate Strikes have also faced criticism from some who argue that young people should be in school rather than protesting or that the strikes are ineffective at achieving substantial policy change.

FUTURE OF CLIMATE JUSTICE

Increasing Renewables

According to a 2022 Survey, most Americans, at least two-thirds, believe the federal government should encourage domestic wind and solar power production. They are divided on whether using electric vehicles and nuclear power production should be encouraged and whether oil and gas drilling should continue. Most people are against continuing coal mining in America (Tyson, 2023). Young people, especially the Woke, are even more invested in a sustainable and safe future, which is why Wokeism makes climate justice issues one of its priorities.

Corporate and Federal Action

Various studies show that most Americans believe that the federal government, elected officials, the energy industry, and large corporations should do more to address the impacts of climate change. But, just over a third of Americans (37%) say addressing climate change should be the top priority for Congress in 2023 (Tyson, 2023). In the Pew Center Research survey on important issues for Americans, climate change ranked only 17th out of 21 national priorities. However, most Republicans and Democrats support smaller measures to impact climate change, saying they would favor a proposal to provide a tax credit to businesses for developing carbon capture and storage technologies (Tyson, 2023).

Overall, the impacts of Climate Justice Movements have raised awareness about the issues and consequences of climate change and the implementation of fossil fuel alternatives. Most people see climate change as a severe problem, but as climate change occurs closer to home, this could drive increased concern and calls for action.

10

WOKE POLITICS

The word woke was hardly mentioned in a political context until 2015, let alone associated with a political ideology called Wokeism (Cohn, 2023). However, Woke movements brought attention to important issues such as police brutality, systemic racism, immigration, criminal justice reform, voting rights, and many other forms of discrimination.

As previously explored, Wokeism sits further on the left of the political spectrum than liberalism and conservativism. It is aligned with the Progressive Left, or as *New York Times* journalist Nate Cohn labels them, the "New Left" (Cohn, 2023). Only 8% of voters belong to this political group; however, they are the most politically active and engaged in conversations about social justice issues, and although a minority, they significantly influence American politics today (Nadeem, 2021a).

Woke politics inherited many characteristics from its leftist, liberal, and progressive origins, especially on cultural and social issues like race, sex, and gender (Cohn, 2023). Their political agendas and grassroots activism were triggered by several key events that have signaled what journalist N.S. Lyons describes as a "Woke Revolution" (Lyons, 2023).

One of the events that galvanized the "woke pushback" on conservative politics was the 2016 election. Trump's campaign, characterized by racist and xenophobic rhetoric, triggered many young people to become more politically active and resist what they saw as a conservative administration's regressive policies and attitudes.

Additionally, Wokeism continued the push for policies that promote diversity and inclusion in workplaces, schools, and other institutions, influencing the shift to a liberal government in the 2020 election. For instance, the Biden administration prioritized diversity and inclusion, appointing a diverse cabinet and signing executive orders to promote equity in government (Ogrysko, 2021).

However, one of the drawbacks of Wokeism's influence on American politics has been the strong push-back by those critical of these sweeping policy changes. While most "anti-woke" critics are conservatives, there are those within the liberals and Democrat ranks that also oppose woke policies and agendas, describing them as "illiberalism" rather than progressive (J. Williams, 2021).

POLITICAL AGENDAS OF THE "NEW LEFT"

Although rooted in the ideologies of progressiveness, the woke "New Left" have their own agendas and methods of political engagement that distinguish them from the progressive liberals who have gone before them.

Purpose of a Woke Government

Traditional conservative politics of the 19th century was based on a government of elected officials implementing enforcement of laws to protect and secure the liberty of individuals from external threats and violence toward each other. In contrast, Progressives saw the purpose of government as not for self-preservation or individual happiness but to redefine freedom as fulfilling human capacity. To "create" individuals rather than to protect them.

Nate Cohn describes how the woke "New Left" continues this agenda and lobbies for increased government intervention to address systemic inequalities and promote social justice that becomes an environment that fosters freedom. This may include policies like affirmative action, government-funded social programs, and regulations to address discrimination (Cohn, 2023).

These initiatives have improved equity and access for many marginalized communities by addressing health, education, climate change, immigration, economic inequality, criminal justice reforms, and other disparities. In addition, the COVID-19 pandemic has highlighted the impact of systemic racism on healthcare outcomes, with BIPOC communities unfairly affected by the virus (Yearby et al., 2022).

Dismantling Oppressive Hierarchies

One of the main drivers of woke politics is to challenge and address the system of overlapping power structures or hierarchies of oppression ingrained in American society at all levels of governance. This stance is the legacy of many decades of social justice reforms. However, it recognizes systemic structures of power, domination, and oppression continue today.

Anti-Liberal

The "New Left" paints a very pessimistic view of liberal progress, saying that it has been inadequate and more radical reforms are required to create meaningful change. Johanna Williams, a critic of Liberalism, believes Liberal politicians have diluted some of the more powerful but polarizing principles and sacrificed equal justice for equal rights. They have adopted compromise solutions to facilitate bi-partisan collaboration on essential issues at the expense of systemic change (J. Williams, 2021).

Genuine Change, Not Compromises

Steven Pinker, in his 2018 book *Enlightenment Now,* challenges this viewpoint and looks to statistical data on overall social trends that show racism, poverty, and discrimination are on the decrease and that diversity, equity, and inclusion policies are working (Pinker, 2018). The "New Left" dispute these claims as over-generalizations because they ignore the negative impacts on marginalized communities. For those engaged in this struggle, it is not data that defines the reality but the lived experience of individuals. Cohn asserts that improvements have occurred for "privileged whites" and "equal rights are a veneer that conceal and justify structural inequality (Cohn, 2023)."

Equity over Equality

The "New Left," although more aligned with liberalism than conservativism, views Liberals' political compromises as instruments obstructing meaningful change. In fact, much of the woke political dialogue opposes liberal "colorblind" values of equal treatment and opportunity because it does not acknowledge that identity consciousness is an integral part of remedying injustice and that there are still unequal outcomes for the marginalized (Cohn, 2023).

The Urgency to Challenge Norms

Cohn also observes that "This does not readily lend itself to a 'politics of hope'" and that virtually everything about America might have to change to end systemic racism (Cohn, 2023). He is skeptical of politicians being effective; rather, it will depend more on individual actions, which explains the urgency of activists "to critique language and challenge norms in everyday life (Cohn, 2023)."

Domestic Policy

William Schambra, a political historian, describes how the role of domestic policy for the original progressive movement was founded on two concerns: First, the government must protect people with low incomes against capitalism through redistribution of resources, anti-trust laws, and regulation of commerce and production. Second, the government should facilitate its citizens' "spiritual" development through promoting art and culture, conservation of the environment, and education (Schambra, 2023). Many aspects of these policies underpin how the "New Left" perceive the role of the government and the structures that support society's progress.

In contrast, conservatives have traditionally seen the government's role to protect citizens and property against violence by instilling laws that police and discipline criminal behaviors. Overall, the intention was for citizens to lead independent, productive lives with minimal government intervention (Schambra, 2023).

Economic Policy

One of the most contentious issues facing the government today is economic policy. The Biden government stated they "will be the first administration ever to construct economic policy around issues like race, gender equality, and climate change, rather than traditional indicators like gross domestic product or deficit ratios (Salmon & Quay, 2021)." Historically, conservative governments focus on economic growth and raising the GDP, and this shift in monetary policy is seen by some skeptics as a token attempt to cater to the Woke and their agenda of wealth distribution for a more just and equitable society (Salmon & Quay, 2021).

In addition, woke critics assert that limiting economic growth will hinder productivity and the goal of increasing wealth for poorer people. Progressives admit that there will still be inequities in wealth with a growth economy. However, everyone will improve their standard of living, not just the wealthy (Salmon & Quay, 2021).

Social Policy

There is a raft of social policies that are promoted by the New Left:

- **Social Justice:** Advocating for policies that address systemic inequalities and promote social justice for civil rights, gender equality, LGBTQIA+ rights, racial and ethnic equality, and disability rights.
- **Healthcare:** Prioritizing affordable and accessible universal healthcare.
- **Education:** Emphasizing the importance of quality education as a means of social mobility, with increased funding for public schools, affordable higher education, and student loan reform.
- **Climate Change and Environmental Protection:** Supporting policies to combat climate change,

transition to renewable energy sources, and preserve the environment.

- **Immigration:** Advocating for more inclusive and humane immigration policies, including pathways to citizenship for undocumented immigrants, protections for refugees and asylum seekers, and the reform of immigration enforcement practices.
- **Criminal Justice Reform:** Prioritizing criminal justice reform to address issues such as mass incarceration and racial disparities in the justice system.
- **Economic Inequality:** Reducing economic inequality through progressive taxation, raising the minimum wage, expanding social safety nets, and implementing regulations to protect workers' rights.

Freedom of Speech

The principle of "Freedom of Speech" is one of the most contentious in the political discourse today. As Cohn describes, The New Left prioritizes politically correct speech over unlimited freedom of speech. This challenges the current framework of free speech, which allows offensive speech because it is not deemed hateful or harmful. Instead, the Woke rejects all speech considered insensitive or harmful enough to trigger vulnerable or marginalized people. They justify this by saying that even in language, there is a privileging of the white concept of "freedom" that is not reflected at the individual level for marginalized people (Cohn, 2023).

As a result, Wokeism is often associated with political correctness, language policing, and bringing accountability to individuals or groups expressing ideas deemed offensive or oppressive. Furthermore, the New Left support creating legal structures and policies to police acceptable language in public domains. This can lead to the suppression and silencing of dissenting views and is seen by critics as restricting free speech and destructive to open discourse (J. Williams, 2021).

Governance by Experts

Disagreement about who should rule the government demonstrates another fundamental difference between progressive and conservative opinions. Schambra describes how, historically, conservatives initially chose elected wise and discerning officials from the general community. Progressives, however, favored well-educated academics and leaders who had the intellectual capacity to advance the movement's political goals. They relied on science, rather than morality, as the necessary instrument for the complex duties involved in the nation's governance (Schambra, 2023).

As a result, the liberalized system of government today reflects many progressive initiatives. The political framework respects the democratic process of electing representatives without serving individual interests and a method of administration intended to create a universal "enlightened bureaucracy" (Schambra, 2023). However, a recent 2022 Pew Research Centre report by Laura Clancy shows that young progressives are willing to forego the democratic process to promote stronger leadership, further instilling fears in conservatives (Clancy, 2023).

Representation in Government

Diversity, Equity, and Inclusion (DEI) are essential progressive values adopted in government since the 1970s, increasing the representation of minority and marginalized groups. Through the subsequent implementation of DEI initiatives in many government areas, at state and federal levels, there have been significant increases in the participation of women and black Americans as elected officials and in administration. However, many Americans on both sides of the political spectrum agree that representation of other racial, ethnic, LGBTQIA+, middle and low-income, and disability groups is lagging. "Without proper representation in our country's legislature, the voices of all citizens are not heard in important decision-making," says the political advocacy organization Common Cause Illinois (Anderson et al., 2021).

Many countries have tried to increase the political representation of marginalized groups through measures like affirmative action and quota systems. However, the New Left believes simply placing a few token representatives in positions of power is not enough to address the systemic barriers that prevent these groups from having an equal voice in decision-making. Furthermore, the New Left now advocate for changes to the electoral process because it disadvantages these minorities, even before they get to the voting booth.

Protecting and Promoting Marginalized Groups

A primary focus for woke politics today is to bring identity issues out in the open, which many believe liberals had downplayed, along with unresolved racial, religious, and partisan issues. This new form of progressive liberalism emphasizes the personal as political. This takes "prioritizing, trusting, and affirming the voices and experiences of marginalized groups" (Cohn, 2023). Identity politics challenges race-neutral (or colorblind) policies and promotes race-conscious ones. This ideological focus is evident in other aspects of society, such as Woke Capitalism and Woke Education.

11

WOKE CAPITALISM

The influence of Wokeism on the corporate world has taken many forms, including public statements of support for social justice movements, donations to organizations, diversity and inclusion training, and even changes in company structure, policies, and investment strategies.

CHANGING THE STRUCTURE OF CAPITALISM

Woke Capitalism is a catchy label for Stakeholder Capitalism. Leading economists such as Professor Klaus Schwab, who founded the World Economic Forum (WEF), assert that traditional shareholder capitalism is not sustainable in a modern economy and that capitalism must be reinvented (Schwab, 2020). Schwab advises that corporate executives must consider interests beyond profit-focus for shareholders to perform in an ethically and balanced, sustainable manner, and instead, advocates that companies should consider more than the owners' or shareholders' interests but include employees, customers, and suppliers (Multiview, 2021).

The Business Roundtable of the top 200 companies agrees,

endorsing the principles of Woke Capitalism. The CEO of JP Morgan, Jamie Diman states: “Major employers are investing in their workers and communities because they know it is the only way to be successful over the long term. These modernized principles reflect the business community’s unwavering commitment to continue to push for an economy that serves all Americans” (D'souza, 2022). Woke Capitalism acknowledges the demand for greater corporate social responsibility in addressing concerns about exploiting marginalized communities and contributing to environmental and social justice issues (Schwab, 2019).

In contrast, those that support shareholder capitalism believe the shareholder's interests should drive and benefit from the company's profits, and losing sight of this will be detrimental to a company’s success (Multiview, 2021). Shareholder capitalism is not necessarily considered socially responsible. However, Milton Friedman, a Nobel Prize-winning economist, argued that capitalism's core, the freedom to engage in entrepreneurial activities, trade goods and services, and make profits for shareholders, is socially responsible. This is because the profits and resources generated bring many benefits to society through jobs, training, and revenue for other suppliers (Friedman, 1970).

Some applaud the initiatives of Woke Capitalism for genuinely promoting and implementing DEI policies and promoting more socially responsible investing (D'souza, 2022). While others, such as Vivek Ramaswamy, are critical of stakeholder capitalism seeing these efforts as tokenistic gestures commodifying Wokeness for financial gain and ultimately sabotaging economic progress (Edesess, 2021; Ramaswamy, 2021).

A WOKE FRAMEWORK FOR CORPORATE RESPONSIBILITY

Embracing Woke Capitalism as a framework involves a commitment to the three pillars of environmental, social, and governance (ESG) responsibilities. These responsibilities have gained increasing international recognition as integral components of sustainable, ethical, and responsible business practices and reflect the influence of woke principles at both the customer and leadership levels (Mathis & Stedman, 2023). ESG encourages companies to measure the risks and opportunities associated with ethical investing and to take a position on specific political issues, even if they have nothing to do with the company's commercial business activities.

Environmental Responsibility

Companies strive to mitigate adverse environmental impacts, promote sustainability, and address climate change as part of their environmental responsibilities. Ecological factors include carbon footprint, waste management, air and water pollution, biodiversity loss, deforestation, and loss of natural resources (Mathis & Stedman, 2023). For example, Patagonia, an outdoor apparel company, recently announced that each year, $100 million in company profits will go to the Holdfast Collective, a U.S. nonprofit working for climate action and policy advocacy. They actively engage in environmental sustainability, reducing their carbon footprint by using organic and recycled materials in their products and advocating for preserving public lands (Auld & Grabs, 2022).

For those who are aware of ESG, a 2021 Morning Consult survey shows that environmental issues are "top of mind," with the majority of Americans (53%) placing this as a top priority (C. Williams, 2021).

Social Responsibility

Social responsibilities involve considering how the company treats different groups of people. This can include addressing diversity, equity, and inclusion within the workforce, ensuring fair labor practices, workplace health and safety, safeguarding human rights, supporting community development initiatives, and engaging in philanthropy (Mathis & Stedman, 2023).

Many big companies responded to woke activism by supporting the Black Lives Matter movement in 2020 (Livingston, 2020). They pledged to address racism and increase diversity and inclusion in their organizations. For example, Nike released an ad campaign that read, "For once, don't do it. Don't pretend there's not a problem in America" (Seth Cohen, 2020).

According to a 2023 survey by Morning Consult, a third of Americans (27%) believe that corporations and CEOs should "Play an active role in communicating their position in and be involved in social and political issues," an increase from 2021 (Tassin, 2023). However, some opinions on "Corporate Wokeism" are that it is mainly performative, and companies should focus on tangible actions and systemic change rather than just rhetoric (Spry et al., 2022).

There can still be risks for companies that take their social justice stance seriously. The woke movement can be polarizing, and companies aligning too closely with these ideals may risk alienating customers or employees who do not share those views (Principato, 2022).

Governance Responsibility

Governance responsibilities focus on maintaining transparent and ethical business practices by adhering to strong corporate governance structures, ensuring board independence and accountability, practicing responsible financial management, promoting anti-corruption measures, and complying with relevant laws and regulations (D'souza, 2022).

The *2020 Davos Manifesto: The Universal Purpose of a Company in the 4th Industrial Revolution* by Klaus Schwab outlines how companies can practice ethical leadership through values such as integrity, fairness, and accountability, which can positively impact their employees, customers, and the wider community (Schwab, 2019).

Woke ideals can also inspire greater creativity and innovation within companies. For example, a diverse workforce may bring a broader range of perspectives and experiences to problem-solving, leading to better outcomes. However, concerns about over-focusing on woke agendas may distract companies from their core business objectives, leading to a lack of innovation or competitive edge (Rugy, 2022a).

Diversity and Inclusion Training

Diversity and Inclusion training programs are tools designed to raise awareness and help employees develop skills for working in a more diverse workplace. They are an essential part of company culture and ESG responsibilities. Many Americans support these initiatives because they believe there are still inequalities within workplaces, especially for black people (Minkin, 2023). For example, Starbucks launched a diversity and inclusion training program for its employees to help them recognize and overcome unconscious bias and promote a more inclusive environment (Tyko, 2020; Washington, 2018).

WOKE-WASHING

"Woke-washing" is the practice of companies or individuals using the language and imagery of social justice activism for marketing purposes without a genuine commitment to social justice principles (Surowiecki, 2023). This practice attempts to capitalize on the growing popularity of social justice movements while avoiding any actual changes necessary to address inequality and discrimination issues. Critics, such as economic analyst Helen Lewis believes woke companies are still driven by economics rather than social responsibility, which she describes as "the iron law of woke capitalism," and claims its benefactors are primarily wealthy, white, well-educated men – not the marginalized (H. Lewis, 2020a).

CRITICISMS OF WOKE CAPITALISM.

There are, however, drawbacks to Stakeholder or Woke Capitalism. Implementing Woke Capitalism can be more complex and challenging, as companies must balance multiple stakeholders' interests. The competing goals of various stakeholders can also lead to decision paralysis within a company, with no clear direction (Denning, 2020). Another flaw that Levine notes is that Woke Capitalism is not sustainable. CEOs rely on public goodwill and sentiment to drive company value, which they will ultimately undermine through corporate greed (Levine, 2022).

Embracing woke ideals can be expensive for companies, especially involving diversity training or recruiting efforts targeted at underrepresented groups. Due to ethical and political concerns, Woke Capitalism may discourage investment and entrepreneurship in specific industries or locations. This may also lead to lower profits and shareholder returns in the short term (Ramaswamy, 2021).

In addition, some diversity initiatives may be seen as tokenistic if they only focus on surface-level changes, such as hiring a few people of color or women in high-profile positions, without addressing underlying issues of bias and discrimination (Rugy, 2022a; Spry et al., 2022). Ramaswamy sees ESG initiatives as a "woke-washing" ploy to appeal to younger and more socially conscious consumers and that "woke-washing" can erode trust in a company's brand and commitments (Ramaswamy, 2021). Distinguishing which companies are engaged in woke-washing with those authentically committed to social justice principles is essential.

Lastly, Mendenhall and Rugy propose that Woke Capitalism hurts the groups it attempts to support and does not advance social justice causes (Mendenhall, 2022; Rugy, 2022b).

Lewis believes in the ideals of Woke Capitalism but is cynical of companies' tokenistic efforts to achieve them: "If you care about progressive causes, then woke capitalism is not your friend. It is actively impeding the cause, siphoning off energy, and deluding us into thinking that change is happening faster and deeper than it really is (H. Lewis, 2020a)." Despite these criticisms, many believe that Shareholder Capitalism has failed and Stakeholder Capitalism is the only way forward (D'souza, 2022). Whereas Denning asserts that both these frameworks have lost sight of the Customer, the only actual driver of economic success (Denning, 2020)

12

WOKE EDUCATION

Progressive ideologies laid the foundation of the modern education system in the 21st century, influencing curriculum content and teaching practices. Addressing issues such as racial and gender equality have had significant impacts in the last decade, particularly in promoting diversity, equity, and inclusion. However, these "woke ideologies" have also been subject to criticism and controversy from conservatives, with some arguing that they promote a narrow and divisive view of social justice. In addition, the increased controversy and politicization of "wokeness in education" have resulted in the passing of anti-woke education laws in various American states.

EVOLUTION OF WOKE EDUCATION

Nancy Kober from the Center on Education Policy provides a broad history of the American education system, which has evolved since the republic's early days to become central to the advancement of society today. When America fought for independence from British rule, a decision was made by political leaders to use the education system to resolve its social issues, unlike European republics that developed welfare systems to handle these concerns (Kober, 2020b).

The Colonial Era

In the early colonial era, education was haphazard and primarily provided by families, churches, and private tutors. Schooling was mainly reserved for white male children and excluded girls and non-white children (Kober, 2020b).

Early National Period

The concept of free, universal education gained prominence, emphasizing the need to educate citizens for democracy. The Northwest Ordinance of 1787 set aside federal land to establish public schools in the territories. Thomas Jefferson proposed a public education system in Virginia. However, many states had no formal school system and relied on the community's charitable support (CEP, 2020).

Common School Movement

After the American Revolution, a public schooling system was designed to support the fragile and newfound democracy by educating people to understand and participate in political and social issues. The school system was also intended to provide "moral instruction and build character (Kober, 2020b)." The new federal government proposed a formal and unified framework of publicly funded schools, with the Common School movement emerging in the 1830s (CEP, 2020).

This strategy involved a standardized curriculum, introducing the 3 R's of reading, writing, and arithmetic. The goal was to educate the poor and middle-class children, to strengthen the nation's economic position, and for the system to work, the progressive reformers argued that children from all social classes must be enrolled. However, there was still strong resistance to including all races and ethnicities (Kober, 2020b).

Progressive Era

By the end of the 19th century, the concept of public schools had spread throughout the country. However, there was still limited access to schooling for girls, children of color, and children with special needs. At the beginning of the 20th century, a new group of progressive educators, led by John Dewey, introduced a student-centered approach to learning, incorporating practical vocational skills in response to increasing industrialization and a growing economy. Kindergartens were introduced for younger children, and attendance in high schools was more regular. Schools became community centers, places of social interaction, and facilities to host various civic activities (Kober, 2020b).

Civil Rights Movement and Educational Reforms

After the Civil War, many states that had previously excluded non-white children from the school system were forced to include them as a condition of entry to the Union. Although compliant, many southern states introduced laws to segregate children of color into separate schools, while American Indian children were forced to assimilate into white schools.

By the mid-20th century, a significant shift in public school reform took place with the promotion of equity and opportunity. Segregation reform in America's schools was brought about through the landmark Supreme Court case Brown v. Board of Education (1954), which declared racial segregation in schools unconstitutional (Kober, 2020b). *The Elementary and Secondary Education Act (ESEA) 1965* provided federal funding to schools serving low-income students. The *Individuals with Disabilities Education Act (IDEA) 1975* mandated equal educational opportunities for students with disabilities (Labaree, 2010).

David Larabee's 2010 book *Someone Has to Fail: The Zero-Sum Game of Public Schooling* describes how during the 1960s and 70s, the Black Power and feminist movements brought greater attention to issues of racial and gender inequality in education (Labaree, 2010). They called for increased representation and inclusion of diverse perspectives in the curriculum. This shift laid the groundwork for the emergence of the progressive ideologies of critical pedagogy and CRT. These concepts introduced sweeping changes in the education system to address systemic inequality and discrimination (NEA, 2021).

CRT and Critical Pedagogy frameworks

Critical pedagogy and CRT are two different but related frameworks. Justus, an advocate of Critical pedagogy, describes it as a child-focused education approach that empowers students to develop critical consciousness and engage in transformative action to challenge and change oppressive social and educational systems (Justas, 2022). It emphasizes the exploration of power dynamics, social justice, and the development of critical consciousness. Critical pedagogy encourages students to question and analyze societal norms, hierarchies, and inequalities and to become social change agents (Adams & Bell, 2016).

In contrast, CRT examines how race and racism intersect with law, policy, and society. These two frameworks have influenced educational practices, policies, and curriculum development, and their legacy is closely related to woke ideology today. Although traditional civil rights movements focussed on incremental change in the education system, CRT introduced radical education reforms that not everyone understood well or endorsed (Delgado & Stefancic, 2017).

Standards-Based Reforms and Accountability

Kober describes how the development of the school system over the preceding decades had resulted in a decentralized welfare system, for those from poor socio-economic backgrounds, with schools providing lunches, counseling, substance abuse prevention, violence prevention, and health care (Kober, 2020b).

Despite these many reforms, the 1983 report "*A Nation at Risk*" raised concerns about the quality of American education, leading to the Standards movement, which emphasized standardized testing and accountability measures. *The No Child Left Behind Act (NCLB)* of 2001 and the subsequent *Every Student Succeeds Act* (ESSA) of 2015 aimed to improve academic performance and reduce achievement gaps (Kober, 2020b).

In parallel, the Choice movement introduced Charter and private school alternatives to traditional public schools to allow parents to choose the path of their child's education depending on their specific social, cultural, or religious preferences (Labaree, 2010). The overarching goal for reform had moved from ensuring access to education to focussing on the quality of education students receive, equipping them with skills and the proper credentials to succeed in a competitive workplace (Kober, 2020b).

WOKE EDUCATION TODAY

The impact of critical pedagogy and CRT on the curriculums of American schools, especially in colleges and universities, has been significant but also controversial. Proponents like Richard Delgado and Jean Stephancic argue that these frameworks promote social justice, equity, and a deeper understanding of historical and contemporary issues. They assert that using CRT's ideas can help understand many issues of "school discipline and hierarchy, tracking, controversies over curriculum and history, and IQ and achievement testing (Delgado & Stefancic, 2017)." They also believe incorporating these frameworks into curriculum and teaching practices can foster inclusivity, empower marginalized students, and challenge systemic injustices through social activism.

On the other hand, critics such as Michael Zwaagstra and Jonathan Haidt argue that these frameworks are ideologically driven, undermine traditional educational values, and lead to the indoctrination of students (Haidt, 2022b; Zwaagstra, 2022). Some states have now passed legislation banning the teaching of CRT in public schools, citing concerns about its perceived divisive nature (Sanzi, 2022; Trimel, 2022).

It is important to note that the discussion around critical pedagogy and CRT is ongoing and evolving. Different scholars and educators may interpret and apply these frameworks in various ways.

Difference between Critical Pedagogy and Critical Thinking

Critical thinking and CRT are often confused or assumed to mean the same thing but are two different educational approaches. Critical pedagogy is an educational philosophy and practice that empowers students to challenge oppressive systems and foster social justice. In contrast, critical thinking is a cognitive process to develop independent and analytical thinking skills to assess information and make informed judgments. Both critical pedagogy and critical thinking are valuable approaches that can complement each other in fostering a deeper understanding of complex issues and promoting social awareness (Brown-Jeffy & Cooper, 2011; Delgado & Stefancic, 2017).

Diversity, Equity, and Inclusion

According to the National Education Association, education systems prioritizing equity and inclusion create more welcoming and supportive environments for students from diverse backgrounds (NEA, 2021). This includes not only racial and ethnic diversity but also diversity in gender identity, sexual orientation, religion, and socioeconomic status (Kober, 2020b). Including policies that promote the participation of students from diverse cultural and ethnic groups is beneficial to academic outcomes. A recent study of 20 universities established a link between diversity and increased academic results. This is because it encourages the quality of the discussions, innovation, and the process of challenging ideas (Crawford, 2022).

Affirmative Action

Affirmative Action policies were initiated during U.S. President Lyndon B. Johnson's administration in 1965 under the *Civil Rights Act*. They were the government's remedy to counter the effects of long-standing discrimination against women and racial minorities, particularly in workplaces and education (Del Pilar, 2023).

As a controversial policy, supporters argued that it protects individuals impacted by historical racism by leveling the playing field and allowing colleges and employers to consider race as a factor in selection processes to support disadvantaged racial minorities. This has increased diversity in higher education, resulting in more diverse leadership in the United States (Harvard Graduate School of Education, 2023). More recently, some university administrators no longer focus on "affirmative action" and "quotas" but embrace "race-conscious" selection processes that, while considering race, also assess other attributes, such as geographic origins, interests, and skills (Del Pilar, 2023).

However, others argue these policies violate equal opportunity principles and promote reverse racism. Instead, they advocate for a "colorblind" approach that ignores race (Ellis, 2023). In universities that have already banned affirmative action policies, a decline in minority numbers has already been observed. The concern is that these actions will further discourage students of color from applying to elite universities, decreasing diversity (Ellis, 2023).

Gender Identity Reforms

Gender reforms in schools have provided safer spaces for children to explore their gender identity and sexual preferences, and as Maria Klawe explains, giving children greater freedom for individualism (Klawe, 2019). Schools and universities have increasingly adopted policies and practices to recognize and support transgender and non-binary students, such as allowing students to use their preferred names and gender-neutral pronouns and providing gender-neutral restrooms (Adams & Bell, 2016).

Some critics are concerned that children are too young to identify with gender until they have reached emotional maturity. They see gender identity as a natural development process, so encouraging children to identify with a gender role too early could stunt their social growth and lead to later psychological issues (Mandelbaum, 2020; Sanzi, 2022).

Challenging Traditional Power Structures:

According to scholars Maurienne Adams and Lee Anne Bell, an approach to teaching that prioritizes social justice and equity can help students critically analyze systems of power and inequality (Adams & Bell, 2016). A woke education can lead to greater awareness and understanding of social issues and encourage students to become agents of change in their communities. For example, when students learn about the history of racism and discrimination, they can better understand the existing systemic barriers and be motivated to work towards dismantling them (Murawski, 2019).

However, education experts say racism is so deeply embedded within the education system that many no longer believe racism exists. Although explicit racism is well recognized and addressed, parents and teachers have been desensitized to implicit bias and racism and its impacts. Progressive educators have called for going beyond racial equity and assert an even more proactive racial justice approach is needed to counter this (NEA, 2021).

Decolonizing the Curriculum

Decolonizing the curriculum involves recognizing and challenging how traditional curricula often reflect and perpetuate colonialism and Eurocentrism and incorporating diverse perspectives and histories into the curriculum. As a result, students from marginalized groups can see themselves represented in the material, which can improve their engagement and motivation (Akomolafe, 2021).

Culturally Responsive Teaching Practices

Culturally responsive teaching is an approach to education that considers students' cultural backgrounds and experiences and uses this knowledge to create a more inclusive and engaging learning environment that can improve academic outcomes for marginalized students (Adams & Bell, 2016).

Holistic Approach

According to Kober, adopting a holistic approach to education systems by prioritizing social and emotional learning can improve students' well-being and academic performance. This approach includes providing students with academic support and addressing their physical, emotional, and mental health needs (Kober, 2020a).

Bridging the Wealth Gap

The wealth disparity in the education system has been a longstanding issue in the United States (Kober, 2020b). It is generally recognized that a person's financial status impacts their resources and opportunities for enrolling in higher education. Some colleges and universities hand out 'merit' scholarships based on test scores, GPA, and extracurricular activities. This situation tips the scale in favor of the wealthy (Whistle, 2020).

In recent years, progressive education systems have addressed economic inequality, including reducing student debt, providing access to affordable housing, and providing resources and support for low-income students (Wolla & Sullivan, 2017). For example, the movement for school funding equity seeks to ensure that all students, regardless of zip code, have access to high-quality education (America Succeeds, 2022).

Many universities and colleges have also implemented programs to increase financial aid for low-income students and address food insecurity and housing instability. These programs aim to provide practical support for disadvantaged students and promote greater social and economic mobility through education (Hillman, 2020).

The 2019 Pew Research Center study on attitudes to education and Gallop Poll findings show that today's public perception of colleges and universities is increasingly negative, particularly amongst Republicans (Mitchell & Parker, 2019). At the same time, Democrats believe things are relatively stable. These results reflect the political polarization around the education system. Some believe this is because most educators at all levels of the education system are liberal. There are fears from conservatives that they over-emphasize liberalism, radical wokeness, and a host of anti-American and anti-social behaviors (Zwaagstra, 2022).

This, however, is not a new perspective. In 2007, the Academic Association of University Professors (AAUP) identified four primary areas of concern about education: Indoctrination, Balance, Hostile Environment, and Relevance, which they addressed in the 2007 report *Freedom in the Classroom* (AAUP, 2007).

Indoctrination

Critics and parents have raised concerns that educators "indoctrinate" rather than "educate"; hence, young adults are being influenced by the most liberal educators to dismiss conservative beliefs, values, and traditional hierarchies. They fear this could lead to a narrow-minded worldview that shuts down open discourse and critical thinking (Haidt, 2022b; Ingraham, 2016).

However, the AAUP dispute this view, and according to a 2020 survey of 100 colleges by IDEALS, students already have relatively fixed political leanings before they attend college and are highly resistant to change (AAUP, 2007; Cooperman, 2023; Rockenbach et al., 2023). Only half of the students surveyed reported that professors frequently expressed liberal views, and the few who felt pressure said it was mainly from teachers who held more conservative views (Rockenbach et al., 2020).

Another national study of 7000 students revealed that most are political Moderates, with little change in political leanings due to their schooling. They were generally "more tolerant of both liberal and conservative views," and they tended to be more influenced by peers than teachers (Altschuler & Wippman, 2023).

Some political observers state that the claims of "woke indoctrination" create an exaggerated fear in some parents and fuel the growing wave of legislation that seeks to intervene in all areas of education (Hammer, 2023). Parents so keenly feel these fears that they prompted one school, The Manhattan Institute, to produce a Woke Schooling toolkit to advise parents on addressing progressive initiatives (Manhattan Institute, 2021).

Balance

Another criticism is the lack of "balance" in the teaching curriculum and methods. Teachers are accused of introducing specific ideologies without exposing students to contrary viewpoints denying them access to a full and fair accounting of a topic (AAUP, 2007).

Concerns have also been raised about the over-emphasis on race, gender identity, and political correctness in schools, leading to division among people from different backgrounds (Mandelbaum, 2020). Furthermore, some fear that woke education goes too far in emphasizing social justice issues, feeling that it threatens free speech and respect for the law and democracy (Manhattan Institute, 2021).

Academics Amna Khalid and Jeffrey Snyder have responded to these claims by asserting that: education's focus is not on teaching "absolute truths" but is instead concerned with critical thinking skills and the pursuit of "truths" which involves inquiry, free speech, artistic expression, and robust discussion for teachers and students (Khalid & Snyder, 2022).

Edward Kirkland, a founding administrator for the progressive education movement in the 1950s, said, "Scholars must be free to examine and test all facts and ideas, the unpleasant, the distasteful, and dangerous ones, and even those regarded as erroneous by a majority of their learned colleagues" (AAUP, 2007).

Academics admit that education is based on a critical pedagogy emphasizing racial and gender disparities and injustices. However, they claim this approach fosters culturally responsive teaching practices, which help children develop a deeper understanding of different cultures and perspectives that prepare them for a globalized world. Teachers also claim that by emphasizing these values and ideas in the classroom, students will grow into compassionate, responsible, accepting, and engaged members of society who are free to express themselves (Brown-Jeffy & Cooper, 2011).

Hostile Environment

There are also concerns that teachers are more intolerant of some students' political, cultural, socio-economic, or religious viewpoints, especially if they do not align with the progressive liberal framework. The concern is that it creates a hostile learning environment for those students from conservative white backgrounds, which can result in reverse racism (AAUP, 2007; Manhattan Institute, 2021).

Censorship

A progressive learning environment promotes anti-discrimination and has codes that suppress offensive speech on racial, sexual, or ethnic grounds. Consideration is now given to religious or political views that should be suppressed, not because of ideological differences, but because those views may threaten vulnerable students when racist, sexist, or gender-phobic. Critics claim this is censorship (Mandelbaum, 2020).

Bullying and Harassment

Another concern is that ideological intolerance promotes bullying and harassment. Students and teachers who don't conform to woke ideology can be publicly shamed and ostracized within the classroom or on social media (Sanzi, 2022). One example involved the assault of a Yale head teacher by his students in 2015 because of unpopular views expressed by his wife (Lindsay, 2020; Mandelbaum, 2020). The concern is that wokeness encourages excessive intolerance, with students responding with hostility and contempt for those who hold views different from their own.

Hypersensitivity

Another concern is the over-emphasis on "safe spaces" and "trigger avoidance," which encourages children to be overly sensitive and easily offended by minor interpersonal transgressions fostering a Culture of Victimhood. This contributes to a lack of resilience and intolerance of different perspectives and ideas (Manhattan Institute, 2021).

Persistent Irrelevance

Persistent irrelevance has also been identified as a primary concern. The introduction of topics such as social activism, gender identity, and other controversial issues are considered by some as inappropriate for classroom discussion, especially in elementary schools, and threaten traditional family values, good citizenship, and patriotism (AAUP, 2007).

There are commonly held standards of teaching outlined in the *1940 Statement of Principles on Academic Freedom and Tenure,* which states that teachers are entitled to freedom in the classroom in discussing subjects of their choice (AAUP, 2006). The AAUP says that teachers can introduce material that may be controversial to illuminate particular ideas or applications but assert that as professional teachers, they can distinguish the difference between "good teaching and "overt propaganda" (AAUP, 2012).

Anti-family Values

Another concern is that woke education promotes anti-family values, such as the breakdown of traditional gender roles and the devaluation of the nuclear family (Manhattan Institute, 2021). Proponents argue that children develop a broader perspective on the world by teaching students about different family structures. They are more likely to appreciate and respect their families' values while valuing others, such as single-parent families or same-sex parents (Adams & Bell, 2016).

Gender Confusion

Some worry that woke education emphasizes gender identity and sexual orientation, which can be emotionally and morally confusing for children. They fear this could lead to a culture of sexual experimentation that is dangerous, leading to further confusion (Zwaagstra, 2022).

Critical pedagogy encourages the examination of societal norms, stereotypes, and biases. For instance, teaching about gender stereotypes has many benefits, such as a more inclusive understanding of gender roles and societal relationships.

Evidence also shows that increased support for LGBTQIA+ youth, including access to resources and support networks, can help children struggling with their identity feel seen and validated (Human Rights Campaign, 2023).

Dumbing Down Education

Lowering Admission Standards

There are more and more examples of universities and colleges adjusting their curricula and standards to attract marginalized students. This can involve removing challenging subjects or lowering admission entry levels. These practices are intended to provide greater accessibility for marginalized students (CBS News, 2021).

However, some say it perpetuates a discriminatory notion that marginalized students do not have the same capacity to meet academic standards as their non-marginalized peers. This may result in lower self-esteem and a lack of confidence in their abilities (McWhorter, 2021b). Some research confirms that lowering admission entry levels can lead to lower academic performance and dropout rates for marginalized students (Black, 2023).

Standardized Testing

Standardized testing is often touted as a colorblind way to measure student achievement. However, research has shown that these tests are often biased against students from marginalized communities, who may lack access to the resources and opportunities necessary to perform well on these exams (Losen & Martinez, 2013).

Tracking

"Tracking" or grouping students by perceived ability is another progressive policy that disproportionately impacts students of color, who are more likely to be placed in lower tracks with less challenging coursework (CBS News, 2021).

Tokenism in Education

In some cases, efforts to increase diversity and inclusion in education may be seen as tokenistic if they only focus on superficial changes, such as adding a few diverse books to the curriculum or hosting a multicultural festival. However, authentic representation in education requires a deeper examination of how the curriculum, teaching methods, and school culture may perpetuate systemic biases and exclude certain groups.

THREATS TO ACADEMIC FREEDOMS

In the current political environment, there are many threats to academic freedom in teaching and learning, which some educators believe leaves education systems in as precarious a state as they were during the McCarthy era of intellectual suppression. Khalid and Snyder, who advocate for academic freedom, identify two broad patterns emerging. From the conservative side, there are external attacks through legislation that govern the content and methods of teaching. From within, threats come from the Left through poorly conceived and executed policies on diversity and inclusion training (Khalid & Snyder, 2022).

In addition, they contend, the strong liberal bias in institutional initiatives within universities and colleges sometimes constrains freedom of speech and debate on these campuses, promoting tensions between administrators, staff, and students.

Anti-Woke Legislation

For many conservatives, education should aim to produce patriotic, civic-minded students. Journalist Suzanne Trimel claims progressive education reforms have threatened and appear to undermine traditional moral values (Trimel, 2022). The threat to the value of patriotism is a common theme that drives the attempt to apply for institutional gag orders through state-based laws.

Since 2021, 18 states have passed laws restricting teachings on race and gender. Some states, such as Iowa, have enacted laws prohibiting teaching CRT and gender identity theory, banning personal pronouns, and limiting gender-separated bathroom use to those of the corresponding biological sex (Trimel, 2022). This move has garnered support from many conservatives. Still, according to an article by Alex Hammer, some activists have "slammed the policies as 'dangerous,' arguing that they promote 'bigotry' toward transgender people" (Hammer, 2023).

Racial and ethnic diversity is also under threat. In 2023, the Supreme Court banned Affirmative Action policies in university admissions, which many woke progressives see as regressive because it threatens the benefits of "race-conscious" selection processes, reinforcing inherent white bias and privilege in the system (Del Pilar, 2023).

FUTURE OF WOKE EDUCATION

Altschuler and Wippman point out that "higher learning has been damaged far more by efforts to correct abuses of freedom than by those alleged abuses" and "education cannot possibly thrive in an atmosphere of state-encouraged suspicion and surveillance (Altschuler & Wippman, 2023)." Alyssa Rockenbach adds, "Americans of all political persuasions should ensure students learn all the essentials of a discipline and engage in constructive dialogue across all ideological boundaries (Rockenbach et al., 2023)."

The overall concern is that woke ideologies, in practice, promote disparity, shame, fear, and intolerance rather than inspiring genuine ideological shifts resulting in positive social actions (H. Lewis, 2020b). Many parents are justifiably concerned about the future of the next generation, and most young people have been exposed to Wokeism through education, media, and advertising by the time they reach elementary school. Although historically, social reforms are initiated through education reform, ultimately, parents are the education system's consumers and decide the outcomes through their vote.

Wokesim has not only become a progressive ideology that influences social reform at a systemic level but has become a controversial motivator to enforce behavioral change at a personal level through weaponizing social media.

13

WEAPONIZING WOKE

Social justice activists began utilizing the reach of online platforms in the last decade to bring accountability and transparency to high-profile individuals and organizations that contravened fundamental human rights. This took the form of publicly outing the offender, known as "calling out" or "canceling," a type of cultural boycotting, which was weaponized as an online vigilante justice system known as "Cancel Culture." Cancel Culture has produced many effective social justice outcomes but has also raised controversy over its methods and damaging impacts on sometimes innocent victims.

A survey by the Pew Research Centre in 2022 found that most people (61%) know of cancel culture, especially younger adults and college graduates. Surprisingly, the number of older people (over 65) aware of cancel culture has doubled in the last few years. Still, despite this growing trend, a quarter of Americans have never heard of cancel culture (Vogels, 2022).

ORIGINS OF CALL-OUT AND CANCEL CULTURE

Watson's article on the *Origins of Woke* describes how six teenage bloggers originated Call-out Culture in the early 2010s, as they documented "problematic things celebrities have done" on their Tumblr blog (Watson, 2020). For many Gen Z, Tumblr was their first real experience with a social media platform allowing people to discuss various topics, from the trivial to the serious.

According to CBS News journalist Christopher Brito, Twitter succeeded Tumblr as the weapon of choice for online advocates, as it has more users, more impact, and provides easier access to celebrities (Brito, 2020). "Canceling" is an extension of "calling out" and is another AAVE slang word from the 1980s that was initially used to show disapproval for a person's actions as a joke or light-hearted criticism.

Culture critic Haaniyah Angus believes that the original bloggers had pure intentions for holding people accountable but that it spiraled out of control in an environment of instant gratification. It subsequently became a tool for "calling out those we do not like," providing the impetus for a practice that evolved beyond genuine advocacy into a more pervasive and divisive trend, which escalated during the pandemic (Angus, 2019).

CANCELING AND CANCEL CULTURE

Canceling is a form of "cultural boycotting" that is one of the most effective tools grassroots social activists utilize to progress social justice. "Cultural boycotting" is an agreement not to amplify, signal boost, give money to or withdraw support publicly in a way that encourages others to follow. Digital media professor Lisa Nakamura says, "People talk about the attention economy; when you deprive someone of your attention, you're depriving them of a livelihood" (CBS News, 2020b).

Cancel Culture weaponized the freedom and reach of social media to allow everyday individuals to bring awareness and accountability to certain problematic behaviors. Personal values and beliefs drive the public expression of disapproval or moral outrage, and the decision to cancel someone is not necessarily because of group outrage or peer pressure.

Prolific advocates, or "social justice warriors," effectively used canceling to bring corporates and institutions to account, create cultural boycotts, reshape policy, and influence governance. But as the practice spread virally and was driven by more personal agendas, it became a breeding ground for various vindictive, spiteful, and abusive comments described as "toxic woke." When the woke platform was used as moral justification to cause physical, emotional, and psychological harm, cancel culture went from being an instrument of social justice reform to a weapon to punish others. This caused many woke activists to distance themselves publicly from the movement (H. Lewis, 2020a).

Those at the extremes of the political spectrum, Liberal Democrats and Conservative Republicans, are the most likely to engage in "canceling" (Atske & Vogels, 2021).

Doxxing

Another method of holding people to account (and punishing them) for problematic behavior is "Doxxing." This practice involves publicly revealing personal information online without consent and is used in some woke activism campaigns. Doxxing is controversial and raises questions about the appropriateness of public shaming and breaching personal privacy (Tan, 2022).

BENEFITS OF CANCEL CULTURE

Accountability

In the 2020 CBS Reports documentary *Speaking Frankly: Cancel Culture,* Meredith Clark and several other media experts examined the impact of Cancel Culture. She said that "canceling can serve a purpose when it gives underrepresented groups the ability to hold the powerful to account" (CBS News, 2020b). It's also a way for the perspectives of people who don't have a voice to be heard and recognized by "punching up." Cancel Culture has empowered everyday people to challenge the status quo and demand accountability from those in positions of power or wealth that harbor racist, sexist, and discriminatory behaviors.

Silencing

Canceling is also a way to silence someone from speaking, especially if their public viewpoints are extremely offensive regarding racist, sexist, or gender-phobic speech towards a particular individual or group and are deemed to be inciting hatred. Canceling on social media can involve "de-platforming" a celebrity or high-profile person. However, Clark says that too often, cancel culture gets obsessed with the purity of someone or an idea, and "if a person doesn't completely align with a set of values, then they are essentially disposable" (CBS News, 2020b).

Real-life Consequences of Canceling

"Canceling" can create severe real-life consequences for those crossing political, social, ethical, or moral boundaries, such as a social media "pile-on," public shaming, boycotting, job firing, or even criminal prosecution.

Clark believes that people who do not have access to power are the most impacted by cancel culture. At the same time, celebrities and the wealthy are most likely to be able to ride out the public backlash. "Getting and staying canceled depends on who you are," she said. In many incidences, cancel culture has been directed at high-profile celebrities like Kevin Hart, Dave Chapelle, Roseanne Barr, and Mel Gibson, but "they can buy their way out of the noise" (CBS News, 2020b).

Many celebrities, artists and authors, and especially comedians make a living out of provocatively challenging social norms through humor, who, although canceled, resume their careers with minimum impact. Other famous people, such as J.K Rowling, have faced the wrath of Cancel Culture for inadvertent comments that were found offensive but have re-engaged in public life once they publicly apologized for their behavior (Janes, 2023).

However, calling out others behavior can also have a serious backlash, bringing their actions into dispute. For private citizens, their subsequent cancellation can haunt them for years.

After a video went viral of Adam Smith berating a Chick-Fil-A employee in 2012 as a protest against the company's anti-gay policies, he received death threats and was fired from his job. He could not gain employment for some years because of his ill-considered choice to post a private video to a few friends that was reposted publicly (CBS News, 2020b).

When asked for feedback from his employer, James Damore, a young Google programmer, wrote a lengthy, well-researched memo on why more men choose high-stress tech jobs than women. There was considerable outrage when his remarks were circulated throughout the company intranet, and he was fired for being sexist (P. Lewis, 2017).

Amy Cooper falsely accused a black man of threatening her while walking her dog. She posted a video describing the alleged attack. The backlash was so severe she lost her high-profile job as an insurance portfolio manager and is now infamous for her racist attitudes (Hurley, 2023).

Amy Cooper's victim, Christian Cooper (no relation), did not condone her racist attitude but expressed concern about the excessive backlash, saying: "I'm not sure someone's life should be defined by 60 seconds of poor judgment" (CBS News, 2020b).

Accountability vs. Punishment

This raises an issue that causes much dissent among Americans today. Because of rising political polarization, there is more and more intolerance for differences of opinion. The reasons why people are "canceled" can sometimes be incredibly trivial, poorly defined, or even wholly unfounded, but are generally justified because they bring accountability rather than punishment (Liu, 2020).

Accountability involves taking responsibility for one's actions and being held responsible for the harm caused by those actions. The goal of accountability is not to punish or shame but to repair the damage that has occurred and prevent it from happening again. It can involve apologizing, making amends, and taking steps to change behavior or address underlying issues. Punishment, on the other hand, is imposing a negative consequence on someone who has exhibited an undesirable or offensive behavior.

Defining accountability or punishment also depends on whether cancel culture is used constructively to identify and redress harm, inspiring positive change, or is a punitive way to exact revenge for wrongful deeds, with no opportunity for learning or forgiveness.

According to the 2022 survey on attitudes to Cancel Culture, most Americans are divided on whether call-out or cancel culture holds people accountable or punishes them. Democrats, black people, and women are more likely to consider canceling positively. But the number of people who believe cancel culture wrongfully punishes people is increasing (Vogels, 2022).

14

TOXIC WOKE

There are many justifiable reasons for "canceling" or "doxxing," and cancel culture has proven to be a powerful means for everyday citizens to address problematic behavior. However, there are growing concerns amongst many Americans that woke has become "toxic," and cancel culture has gone too far because the potential harm it can cause outweighs the original transgression and can circumvent the systems of legal justice and due process. Moreover, these actions contradict woke principles of empathy and understanding because they often fall short of these ideals (Liu, 2020).

Unfortunately, some individuals weaponize woke ideology and tactics as a subterfuge to inflict harm on those they dislike or disagree with, irrespective of ideological or political differences, just because they feel self-righteous and justified. Conversely, being Woke can make someone a target. One journalist from *The Washington Post*, Molly Roberts, cynically believes woke has been reduced to mean: "I just don't like you (Roberts, 2023)." There are several ways woke is weaponized as part of this toxic behavior:

- Trying to get someone fired, expelled from school, or socially ostracized because they say or believe some different opinion.
- Treating minor slights, mistakes, or non-woke viewpoints as evidence that someone holds deeply bigoted views or is immoral.
- Attempting to spread the word that this person has offensive beliefs, apparently to "protect" others.
- Organizing a mob to harass the person online and sometimes offline as well.
- Canceling people who refuse to participate in shunning another canceled person (Campbell & Manning, 2018).

CYBER BULLYING

Woke culture becomes toxic when online engagement becomes harassing, bullying, and threatens or causes physical harm. As a result, it can have serious negative consequences for the mental health and well-being of those targeted (Liu, 2020).

When cancel culture is weaponized and used to attack individuals simply for expressing an opinion or holding an unpopular belief, some believe it is a real threat to democracy and free speech (Ekins, 2020). Critics say the process stifles free expression, inhibits the exchange of ideas, and keeps people from straying from their comfort zones. It can also lead to a mob mentality and groupthink (Barg, 2020). However, many progressives do not support or condone these toxic behaviors, and ironically, activists are sometimes censored for expressing "anti-cancel culture" opinions, as the CBS documentary *Speaking Frankly* explains (CBS News, 2020a).

The tendency to engage in personal attacks and character assassination is common in cancel culture but is not limited to online interactions. In some cases, activists have resorted to physical violence to silence their opponents. For example, in 2019, journalist Andy Ngo suffered a brain hemorrhage when he was attacked by Antifa activists while covering a protest in Portland, Oregon (CNN, 2019; Smith, 2021). This violence is antithetical to the woke principles and undermines the Woke movement's legitimacy.

Experts consider, in the context of social justice activism, it is essential to consider the potential harm to innocent individuals through public shaming and accountability measures and to ensure that they do not violate an individual's privacy and safety (Tan, 2022).

SOCIAL MEDIA SHAMING

Twitter has been accused of being one of the worst platforms for its toxic culture of abuse. Cathy O'Neil, author of *The Shame Machine*" has described it as a "Shame Network" (O'Neil & Baker, 2022). Journalist Charlie Warzel says shame can be "a healthy, cohering influence that enforces norms and provides accountability on social media," but highlights how social media platforms encourage a "Twitter pile-on," not to promote social justice but to engage a larger audience for its algorithms, that ultimately is focused on making money (Warzel, 2023).

CENSORSHIP

Another criticism of cancel culture is its tendency to moral relativism and intolerance for differing opinions, which results in censorship (Atske & Vogels, 2021). One example of this is the controversy surrounding journalist Bret Stephens. In 2019, Stephens wrote an op-ed for The New York Times expressing skepticism about the global climate crisis. Activists accused Stephens of being a "climate denier," the response was swift and severe, with some calling for him to be fired, arguing that his views were dangerous and harmful (Sheth, 2017).

This kind of reaction to dissenting opinions is not unique to the climate change debate. In many other areas, individuals who express views that challenge the prevailing woke viewpoint can be subject to intense scrutiny and backlash. As a result, many are hesitant to express their anti-woke opinions for fear of being labeled as "immoral" or "bigoted" (Liu, 2020).

DIVISION

Some critics of Wokeness believe it promotes divisiveness rather than fostering unity and progress. By focusing so heavily on social identities, woke culture reinforces these identities, which can contribute to a sense of tribalism, perpetuate stereotypes, and diminish the overall effectiveness of political engagement, creating further divisions between groups (Bowman, 2023).

Some say overemphasizing "forced diversity" causes divisiveness and cultural clashes between marginalized and non-marginalized groups. For example, some felt the casting of Halle Bailey, an African American, as Ariel in Disney's live-action adaptation of "The Little Mermaid" was tokenistic and disrespected the source material, as an example of "wokeness gone too far" (Romano, 2022).

CULTURE OF VICTIMHOOD

Others point to the over-emphasis on language and the prevalence of "political correctness" in woke culture for encouraging hypersensitivity and an overreliance on language policing. As a result, individuals become overly concerned with microaggressions and other perceived slights and react disproportionately to being offended, cultivating a Culture of Victimhood and Entitlement, which has been ridiculed by the anti-woke as "For Me Culture" (Campbell & Manning, 2018; Friedersdorf, 2015).

TRIBALISM AND GROUPTHINK

Another concern about woke culture becoming toxic is a tendency towards groupthink, when individuals conform to the group's views rather than engaging in independent thought or critical analysis. This can limit innovation and progress, stifling dissenting voices and promoting conformity rather than intellectual diversity. Although tribalism occurs amongst many online groups, irrespective of political agenda (Haidt, 2022a).

OPPRESSION OLYMPICS

While Wokeism supports dismantling external hierarchies in society, it can create tensions and in-fighting within BIPOC, and LGBTQIA+ communities. The "Oppression Olympics" is a term that describes "intersectional infighting" between these marginalized groups. While intersectionality is a way of understanding how different forms of oppression compound one another, some argue that it has been co-opted by certain groups who use it to prioritize some forms of oppression over others (Pender Greene, 2022).

For example, the MeToo movement was initially embraced by many as a powerful force for change. However, as the movement gained momentum, it became the target of criticism within feminist and LGBTQIA+ communities. Some felt it had gone too far in its efforts to police interpersonal relationships and sexual conduct (Copeland, 2021).

MORAL SUPERIORITY

The emphasis on purity and perfectionism that can emerge in Wokeism can also lead to a sense of moral self-righteousness and judgmentalism. In some cases, this can create an atmosphere of pressure and anxiety for vulnerable people to navigate. A vocal anti-woke critic Bari Weiss points out that individuals who don't conform to the woke ideal may feel ostracized or marginalized, even if they are sympathetic to the movement's broader goals (Weiss, 2021).

MORAL RELATIVISM

Moral relativism can manifest as an "ends justify the means" mentality, where individuals are willing to overlook or justify bad behavior if they feel it serves a moral cause. This can lead to a situation where otherwise well-intentioned and compassionate individuals engage in harmful and abusive behavior toward others. This thinking is dangerous, as it can dehumanize individuals by relating to them as mere obstacles to social justice.

According to Cohn, the moral righteousness that has emerged in the voice of the woke generation has a sense of urgency and moral clarity (Cohn, 2023). However, one of the most pernicious aspects of toxic Woke culture is how this can lead to moral relativism.

The writer and activist Roxane Gay reflected on this behavior in a 2021 opinion piece: "Online we want to be good, to do good, but despite these lofty moral aspirations, there is little generosity or patience, let alone human kindness (Gay, 2021)."

Political journalist Molly Roberts also observed how social media was initially used to express moral outrage but lost the ability to "distinguish between self-righteousness and righteousness, between virtue-signaling and virtue (Roberts, 2023)."

TOTALITARIANISM

Wokeism has even been labeled by some as "the very definition of totalitarianism," which generally refers to a system of government where the state has complete control (Barg, 2020). It suppresses dissent, restricts individual freedoms, and seeks to control all aspects of society, a concept antithetical to most Americans who value liberty and democracy.

While the influence of Wokeism may sometimes be overstated, critics are concerned that pursuing specific social equity goals may lead to an expansion of state power and government intervention. They suggest that an overemphasis on social justice could potentially result in a loss of individual liberties and the consolidation of power in the hands of a few. Some conservatives fear it is the ultimate agenda of Wokeism, or at least exaggerate and promote that fear, as a justification for opposing and undermining the woke agenda (Graham, 2023).

WOKE AS THE JOKE

Being woke in the early millennium brought a sense of pride. It was a compliment to describe individuals, especially in the African American community, actively working towards creating a more equitable society. The groundswell of support for Wokeism reached a height after the global response to George Floyd's murder.

However, a shift in the perception of woke started after the 2016 presidential election campaign, and the increase in performative Wokeness attracted criticism, ridicule, and scorn.

TOKENISTIC GESTURES

The prevalence of fake activism, "hashtag activism," and "virtue signaling" was seen as tokenistic gestures that discounted and dismissed the actions of genuine social justice activists. It includes Woke individuals publicly expressing their support of social justice issues but privately espousing different views. Journalist Derek Thompson has labeled this practice “front yard politics (Thompson, 2023).” It looks good out the front but hides the “bigoted views” out the back.

PSEUDO-INTELLECTUALISM

Wokeism has also been dismissed as a “radical left-of-center ideology” for pseudo-intellectuals who espouse theory without understanding it. Less educated and disadvantaged woke supporters have limited access to unbiased information and come to rely on the media for facts. Social media has become a free-for-all of random posts from self-styled experts on politics, the law, and health, to spruik various unfiltered opinions, conspiracy theories, and pseudo-science that many young people quickly embrace. This further erodes the credibility of Wokeism and makes it an easy target (Umeadi, 2016).

REDUCTIONISM

Some people are concerned that progressive ideologies encourage individuals to rely more on emotions and feelings than on critical thinking skills and factual evidence to guide inquiry, debate, and drive actions. The social media environment of fake news and sensationalism provokes emotional rather than intellectual responses. Therefore, complex issues are reduced to simplistic terms, such as "systemic racism" or "white privilege," which can lead to a lack of nuance and understanding. Reductionism has increased as political activism has engaged a broader base of less educated supporters (Brubaker, 2020).

HYPOCRISY

The inability to distinguish between self-righteousness and righteousness has made some Woke activists an easy target for comedians and satirists. Roberts notes how they pounce on any "whiff of woke" to write off a wide range of efforts to address inequality, serious and unserious alike (Roberts, 2023).

Dave Chapelle, is widely recognized as one of the most influential comedians of his time for addressing sensitive topics, such as race, politics, and social justice, with a blend of humor and thought-provoking insights. His comedy often challenges conventional thinking and offers a perspective that encourages audiences to reflect on societal norms and taboos. However, he, too, has been subject to harsh criticism for his insensitive and transphobic references in his recent Netflix series (Janes, 2023).

Using humor has been a subtle way for anti-woke critics to undermine Wokeism by mocking its inconsistencies and hypocrisies and baiting naïve young activists, initially in the name of "good fun." But linguistics expert Jeffrey Barg suggests this has created an opening for far-right critics to capitalize on anti-woke sentiment. In recent years, the increased awareness of anti-racism has forced white people to face some uncomfortable truths and their own "white fragility." He suggests that many conservatives and liberals find some woke anti-racism reforms too extreme, so it's far easier to attack the ideology of Wokeism as flawed or aberrant than appear overtly racist (Barg, 2021).

As a result, many woke activists believe it is vital to reconnect "woke culture" with its original principles of challenging dominant narratives and stereotypes and advocating for systemic change. Unfortunately, recent backlash against Wokeism has escalated from mocking into a full-on assault, with right-wing conservatives declaring a "War on Woke!"

15

THE WAR ON WOKE

Over the last decade, political participation by Americans has increased. As early as 2012, Jonathan Haidt, a professor of business studies, observed that for the first time in American political history, Democrats and Republicans had sorted themselves into a perfect left-right split, calling the result a 'dangerous era' in U.S. politics (Pappas, 2012). Over the last few years, these tensions have escalated into what is called Reactionary politics and recently dubbed by the media as the 'Culture Wars" between Republicans and Progressives. Concerns are fuelled by the 2024 election campaigning that some fear could erupt in violent upheaval, not unlike the volatile political environment of the late 19th century (Waldman, 2017).

Although Wokeism was initially dismissed as a "Gen Z trend," its influence on social reforms and sway over more prominent community sections is now taken more seriously by older conservatives. Jeffery Barg believes woke has become too mainstream too fast, allowing it to be coopted by the right and re-engineered as an insult, "which is how the right adopted woke as a favored bogeyman (Barg, 2021)."

However, *Politico* journalist Jon Grinspan optimistically interprets this as a time of awakening from political ambivalence, which is not necessarily bad. Political engagement is higher, and more people turn out to vote and take active ownership over shaping the country; however, he notes that it awakened an old antagonistic approach to political debate, and "woke" is on the firing line (Grinspan, 2021).

HISTORY OF POLITICAL CONFLICT

Grinspan believes the current situation is reminiscent of the years of political turmoil between the Civil War and the early 1900s when politics was "far more unruly, violent and corrupt than it's been before or since." It was a period when millions of Americans turned out to protest, and political violence was so extreme that thousands of people died, and three presidents were assassinated. At the time, one populist newspaper reported: "We are the worst governed country on the face of the earth" (Grinspan, 2021).

After the upheavals of the Civil Rights era, Americans enjoyed a period of political calm for many decades, where voter turnout was modest, and governments focused on the process of running the country. Conservatives, Moderates, and Liberals populated all political parties. They were willing to cross the floor on moral or ideological grounds, even if it went against party policy.

Ideological Differences

Liberals and conservatives often have divergent views on the role of government, individual rights, and the appropriate balance between social equality and personal liberty. Liberals tend to support a more active role for the government in addressing social and economic issues. At the same time, conservatives generally advocate for limited government intervention and prioritizing individual freedoms. The ongoing debate over the size and scope of government involvement in healthcare, taxation, and education highlights these ideological differences.

Both liberals and conservatives engage in political strategies that can exacerbate tensions. For example, using negative campaigning, obstructionism, and wedge issues to mobilize their respective bases can create a hostile and divisive political environment, hindering effective governance. But in the last three decades, there has been a gradual return to the prominence of extreme right politics globally.

Bart Cammaerts, a political scientist, proposes this resurgence is a reaction to the predominant progressive liberal politics that dominate government frameworks today. In his paper, *The abnormalization of social justice,* he explores how "metapolitics," a system of political tactics favored by fascist groups, is now being used by right-wing extremists. He says the aim is to create a "War of Position," which subtly normalizes viewpoints generally seen as morally corrupt, such as racism, sexism, and fascism, which "over time, if reinforced, becomes the new norm, unquestionable and beyond debate (Cammaerts, 2022)."

Metapolitics and the War of Position

Metapolitics has been hijacked by the extreme right by appropriating woke concepts of class and identity politics and flipping them on their heads. They denounce genuine democratic struggles for gender, racial and sexual equality as a "Woke Revolution," portraying it as anti-democratic, unpatriotic, and immoral (Cammaerts, 2022).

The political divide between the Woke Progressives and Conservatives is no longer just about ideological differences. The media focuses on gender and identity politics as the cause of a significant cultural rift in morals and traditional values and portrays this as "polarized." However, differences in attitudes towards controversial issues, such as abortion, LGBTQIA+ rights, and immigration, also contribute to these tensions. The conflict reflects deeper values and belief systems, leading to disagreements on personal autonomy, morality, and societal norms that are weaponized by politicians and activists from both sides, polarizing the debate further.

Pew Research Centre Polls on political typologies confirm that political polarization and division are being led by "Faith and Flag Conservatives" against the "Progressive Left" or "The Woke" (Nadeem, 2021b). However, this division is not based on racial differences. Most black people are religious Moderates, more likely to support anti-racism and diversity but less supportive of gender identity politics. The divide is mainly driven by class and politics, not race. The battle lines have been drawn between two specific socio-political groups: white, male, religious, less affluent country people, and white, well-educated, wealthy city people.

Oversupply of a Super-rich, Ultra-educated Elite

Peter Turchin, in his 2023 book *End Times* proposes, however, that the real issues impacting American society are driven by economics and the declining fortunes of middle-class Americans and an elite overproduction, where "society produces too many superrich and ultra-educated people, and not enough elite positions to satisfy their ambitions (Turchin, 2023)."

Lewis also stresses that economics significantly influences

political divisions more than social justice issues, which are a smokescreen for more pressing concerns (H. Lewis, 2020b). Moderates are being targeted by both parties exaggerating controversial issues to swing their vote. This Reactionary Politics is popularized and driven by online media and social platforms that monetize this "cultural war."

REACTIONARY POLITICS

"Reactionary," according to political journalist Sam Tanenhous, means an "organic response to political and social revolution, and the relatively reasonable fear that the shared common life of a people has been "wrenched out of its cherished ideals (Tanenhaus, 2016)."

Many social issues are plaguing America and the world: rising poverty, climate change, an inadequate educational system, national unrest, and increased violence. The pandemic only accentuated these issues. The respectful debate between political opponents has devolved into an environment where people are instructed daily that the other side is not only wrong but downright evil (Waldman, 2017). Wokeism may seem immoral for many conservatives and too "PC" for some liberals. Still, where once politicians invoked a war on communism, fascism, or terrorism, they have now waged a "War on Wokeism."

These differences in underlying moral and ethical values underscore their political position. For example, the controversy surrounding issues like same-sex marriage or transgender rights emphasizes the moral and religious divide between progressives and conservatives, who hold more traditional values. Lyons asserts that Republican politicians even go as far as to say democracy is at risk and civil war is imminent (Lyons, 2023). This is a highly charged environment where people stop listening to each other, stop caring, and dehumanize the people on the "other" side.

THE RISE OF ANTI-WOKEISM

The rise in Anti-Wokeism traces back to the 2010s when social justice movements began to gain momentum in the mainstream media. However, as they gained more visibility, influence, and popularity, they became the targets of conservative criticism and backlash.

Genuine woke activism has been, and continues to be, embraced by "good faith actors," prioritizing actions that bring about social change and promote equity and justice. However, some believe the actions of "bad faith actors" have undermined and misrepresented the core principles and goals of the woke movement.

In 2021, Conservatives became increasingly reactive to what it described as "wokeness," which broadly meant any attempt to engage in civil rights or social justice. By 2022, Anti-Wokeism had become an ideology in itself, in what some cynical observers saw as an attempt by the right to rebrand bigotry as a heroic resistance movement (Harriot, 2022).

Conservatism

At the core of Anti-Wokeism, Conservatism values traditional hierarchies. It prioritizes protecting the individual and their property rights, with limited government intervention in education, economy, or social structure. Conservatives feel strongly about group loyalty, betrayal, hierarchy, authority, and sanctity and perceive Wokeism as threatening established cultural norms and values (Pappas, 2012).

While some Conservatives acknowledge the existence of discrimination, they may approach it differently from Progressives, focusing on individual efforts rather than systemic solutions.

Fundamentally, they resist the speed and extent of social justice reforms throughout politics, education, corporations, and workplaces.

The Alt-Right

Beyond the "anti-woke" is a prominent and vocal group of extreme right political activists called the Alt-right or "Faith and Flag Conservatives," who reject the ideology and actions of woke activism wholeheartedly and are the most diametrically opposed to the Progressive Left.

The "Alt-right" is a far-right political movement that emerged in the United States in the late 2000s. It is characterized by white nationalism, anti-Semitism, and opposition to multiculturalism. The movement gained momentum during the 2016 presidential election and Donald Trump's campaign rhetoric that appealed to Alt-Right values. Key group members were profiled in a 2020 documentary called *White Noise* by journalist Daniel Lombroso for *The Atlantic* (Lombroso, 2020).

The Alt-Right has been highly critical of woke progressives, whom they see as threatening American culture and values. They also believe Wokeism demonizes white men and stifles free speech. The Alt-Right is one of the highest political user groups on social media and has been associated with online harassment campaigns of pro-woke activists and promoting racist and gender-phobic hate speech.

The "Alt-right" pushback on Wokeism has focussed on reverse racism, denial of systemic racism, and white nationalism.

Alt-Right Agenda

Alt-right supporters have argued that woke ideology promotes "reverse racism" or "anti-white" discrimination. Anti-woke critics such as Ben Shapiro accuse Wokeism of more than dismantling traditional hierarchies of oppression but have flipped them so that white people are now the oppressed and minorities are the oppressors. Others accuse Wokeism of promoting a "hatred for white people" and have called it a form of "anti-white supremacy" (Harriot, 2022).

With the emergence of the "War on Woke," Deberry describes how "bending" the language was "a game that conservatives have played for a long time" and how every Black critic of racism has been called a racist in return (Deberry, 2021).

The Alt-right has often rejected the idea that systemic racism exists in American society. Alt-right leader Mike Cernovich's 2017 interview with CNN argued that claims of systemic racism were "a form of victimhood that people are using to gain power." Similarly, far-right advocate Milo Yiannopoulos has claimed that "systemic racism is a myth" and has accused those who promote the idea of being "anti-white racists" (Lombroso, 2020).

Alt-right leader Richard Spencer has openly embraced white nationalism in response to the perceived threat of Wokeism and declared that "a white ethnostate is the only way to avoid the racial conflicts tearing America apart" (Dart, 2016).

THE "CULTURE WAR" TACTICS

The "Culture War" is a "war of position," which Cammaerts believes is framed as a "woke vs. anti-woke" battle of democratic, patriotic, and religious values, which undermines prevailing social and political systems in America (Cammaerts, 2022).

While the Alt-right has attempted to detoxify their culture of racism, sexism, homophobia, and transphobia, Conservative

Republicans have also taken up the "war of social reform." However, to do so, there must be a prominent "enemy," not just an ideological outsider, but one that Cammaerts describes as impure, deviant, and must be rejected.

The Anti-Woke culture war is being driven and amplified by right-wing media, through two main strategies, according to Cammaerts:

- to alienate or "other," those that "actively counter racist, sexist, and anti-LGBTQIA+ views, and fight for social justice;
- and cultivating white victimhood by denouncing cancel culture and weaponizing free speech (Cammaerts, 2022).

Amplifying Fear

Identity politics is highly polarised and over-policed by "moral entrepreneurs" with a raft of unfiltered ideological opinions, which, as Cammaerts asserts, are consistently amplified by the Alt-Right media. They disproportionately focus on gender reforms in elementary education, conveying that the woke movement is more powerful and threatening than it is (Cammaerts, 2022). Angus points out that many engaged in these online conversations don't realize that the impact of hate speech is over-exaggerated and that social media itself, although a valuable tool for drawing attention to issues, can "only do so much (Angus, 2019)."

"Othering" and Abnormalization

"Othering" is defined as a "set of dynamics, processes, and structures that engender marginality and persistent inequality across any of the full range of human differences based on group identities (Powell & Menedian, 2017)." The media and "moral entrepreneurs" play a pivotal role in turning behaviors, ideas, or groups of people into deviant through labeling and stigmatization (Cammaerts, 2022)." This, in turn, fosters negative attitudes towards those people and creates what is called "horizontal out-groups." In particular, those denoted as "The Woke" are separated from what conservatives consider "The American People." Cammaerts believes that the Alt-right anti-woke stance is winning the "War of Position" and that anti-woke ideology has become the new norm.

Cammaerts also believes that social justice struggles, such as anti-racism, or pro-LGBTQIA+ rights, are conveniently labeled and stigmatized as extremist, destructive, intolerant, anti-democratic, and authoritarian. In addition, Those who espouse such opinions are part of "extreme cultural and political groups" that are crazy, elitist, irrational mobs "lacking a sense of humor and out of touch with common sense (Cammaerts, 2022)."

A New Commonsense

The attempt by the Alt-right to reposition white extremist ideology as the new norm also uses the strategy of delegitimizing Wokeism as ridiculous or illogical and describing discriminatory actions as the new normal or "just plain commonsense (Cammaerts, 2022)."

These are old arguments given new life. Typically, one person accuses another of being racist and is then accused of reverse racism. This includes being judged as oversensitive, exaggerating, illogical, and generally "seeing racism where there is none (Cammaerts, 2022)." Therefore, dismissing what is initially an appropriate response to the offensive, racist speech or actions into a social infraction that gets treated more seriously than the original racist remarks.

Moral Panic

In 1972, sociologist Stan Cohen first defined the concept of moral panic in his book *Folk Devils and Moral Panics*: "A condition, episode, person or group of persons emerges to become defined as a threat to societal values and interests; [...] the moral barricades are manned by editors, bishops, politicians and other right-thinking people (Stanley Cohen, 2002)."

French writer Alex Mahoudeau's book "The Woke Panic" deciphers this phenomenon in modern times and claims that "any discourse perceived as radical and violent, questioning the relationships of hierarchy and domination" is labeled as "Wokeism." Stephane Foucart adds that a moral panic is created when Wokeism is portrayed as a danger "that undermines democracy and the Republic" that "prepares the march toward totalitarianism," manufacturing good reasons to be afraid (Foucart, 2022).

The Anti-Woke are accused of adopting this strategy; for instance, John McWhorter, in his book *Woke Racism*, openly accused "Woke" as fanatical, racist, and elitist and likened it to a fundamental religion or cult (McWhorter, 2021b). A Republican senator recently likened woke to a disease and insisted Wokeness was to blame for the massacre of 19 young children in Texas because "schools no longer teach good values" and students are being "infected with woke indoctrination" (Roberts, 2023).

Furthermore, frequently associating the word "mob" with "woke" invokes a vision of irrationality, disobedience, and vindictiveness, all commonly associated with the real threat of an angry and dangerous mob.

White Victimhood

This reverses the perceived roles of perpetrator and victim so that White people now claim they are victims of a system that discriminates against them. In her 2018 book *White Fragility*, Robyn DiAngelo stresses this point: "Racism becomes about white distress, white suffering, and white victimization," and attempts to shift the responsibility of relieving white discomfort back onto the black people who have been the ones most adversely impacted by racism (DiAngelo, 2018).

Difference between Free Speech and Speech That Harms

One of the central issues in the "Cultural Wars" is the right to free speech and the over-emphasis by the progressive left on policing political correctness in language. Critics claim the mindset of the Woke has become punitive rather than instructive. Roberts describes how a new set of language norms have been created that polite society is expected to follow and understand. You can face severe consequences if you get it wrong (Roberts, 2023).

The Alt-right weaponizes their right to free speech and considers their views on discrimination and racism no different from anti-racism or anti-sexism, attempting to legitimize "hate speech" as a debatable opinion. If anyone contests this, then they are the ones who are denying the right to free speech (Cammaerts, 2022). Constructing "racism versus antiracism" as two opposing opinions worthy of debate disregards the generally held belief in society that hate speech and racism are inherently unethical and unconstitutional.

These attitudes are not just political positions but are now influencing real-world actions.

After a loss to the Democrats in the 2020 election, Republicans were anxious to win back the White House, and candidates began to look for a new leader for the anti-woke movement. They found one in Ron DeSantis, the Florida Governor, who authored the *Stop Woke Act* (Contreras, 2023).

His was the first of many legislative actions nationwide to prevent educational institutions and businesses from teaching anything that would cause anyone to "feel guilt, anguish or any form of psychological distress" due to their race, color, sex, or national origin. Despite being framed as a "colorblind" policy, this bill targeted Critical Race Theory and the diversity and equity training that made white people uncomfortable. A federal judge considered some of the bill's intentions "positively dystopian" and had it amended (Harriot, 2022).

The Guardian journalist Michael Harriot wrote that this moment in modern political history is when anti-woke became a mixture of McCarthyism and white grievance (Harriot, 2022). DeSantis even took on Disney, one of Florida's largest employers, and declared it a woke enemy of the state where "Woke goes to die" (Pierce, 2023).

A clear sign that the Republican pushback was real came a few months later when US Supreme Court overturned Roe vs. Wade, ending constitutional protection for abortion rights in the United States, and Affirmative Action was banned in 2023. Foucart thinks the real danger to democracy is not the Woke but rather the extreme right, who, encouraged by their assault on the white house, are now attacking democracy rather than defending it (Foucart, 2022).

Since the lead-up to the 2024 presidential elections, the Republican party campaign focused on Wokeism as the new "evil" to overcome. Some believe Republicans use Wokeism as a metaphor to describe any policy or practice that they do not like (Roberts, 2023). Political opponents are not seen as people with a different point of view but as evil, where debates are no longer disagreement; they're treason (Pappas, 2012).

In contrast, woke supporters see the coalition of Republicans, right-wing judges, and "Make American Great Again" (MAGA) activists as an expression of white Christian Nationalism that displays contempt for the Constitutional First Amendment definition of Free Speech (Rubin, 2023).

Despite this "War on Woke" campaign by the Republicans, a recent Ipsos/USA Today poll found that most Americans (56%), including many Republicans (37%), still view wokeness in favorable terms, defining it as being "informed, educated on, and aware of social injustices." In comparison, a smaller number of Americans (39%) still view it rather benignly for "being overly politically correct and policing others' words." Most do not view woke as dangerous or threatening (Pierce, 2023).

Education Bans

Republicans now use "woke" as a catchall for liberal excess. Ironically, while one of their main criticisms of Wokeism is its focus on gender issues, these have become central to the Republican platform. Legislation that targets state colleges' diversity and inclusion programs is underway in many states to ban classroom discussions on gender identity and sexual orientation (Knowles, 2023).

Another contentious issue in education is the banning of books. While children's books that discuss gender issues have not been well received or broadly endorsed, the efforts to ban books criticizing historical racism may have backfired. A national CBS News poll found that overwhelming majorities of Americans believe that books should never be banned for criticizing U.S. history or discussing race and slavery (Pierce, 2023).

On the contrary, the Ipsos/ USA Today poll showed that most people surveyed said schools should be allowed to "teach about ideas and historical events that might make some students uncomfortable," with many saying that public schools teach too little about Black history and doing so would help students "understand what others went through" (Pierce, 2023).

Corporate Battlefield

The Anti-woke strategy includes taking on big business, with a proposal to ban the consideration of environmentally sustainable and socially conscious investing frameworks. This is based on a claim that ESG is an insidious form of "Woke Capitalism" that will undermine the country's economy. This is despite Stakeholder capitalism being the earliest form of corporate governance in the early 20th century and regarded by many economists as superior to Shareholder Capitalism. Moreover, industry surveys do not validate these efforts either, which report that most Americans do not even know what ESG investing is. When informed on what it entails, most believe financial managers should consider these ESG matters when investing (Pierce, 2023).

Anti-woke Legislation

A raft of Anti-woke legislation is being tested in courts throughout America. Anti-CRT laws invest state legislatures with extraordinary powers to regulate public colleges and universities' curricula. As a result, they directly threaten the academic freedom principles central to teaching, including the autonomy of faculty to choose the curricula and course content (Khalid & Snyder, 2022).

DeSantis has been effective with the so-called *"Don't Say Gay"* law, which prohibits discussing sexual orientation or gender identity in classrooms from kindergarten through to third grade, which he is now seeking to expand to all grades. Several other states are following suit. However, in a 2022 ABC News/Ipsos poll, most Americans surveyed said they opposed such a policy (Pierce, 2023).

Although the Trump administration appointed several conservative judges to the District and Federal courts, one refused to uphold a "drag queen ban" proposed by MAGA Republicans in Tennessee because it was unconstitutional. A conservative judge's fairness in this ruling assures that impartiality prevails in assessing these cases (Rubin, 2023).

Roberts suggests that conservatives' obsession with wokeness will backfire and reignite a strong response, just as the overzealousness of liberals and progressives has sometimes undermined their political agendas (Roberts, 2023). Although this process of rebalancing the political extremes will tend to reach an equilibrium, overall, the trend in American society is toward a more progressive, educated, racially diverse, and less religious culture.

16

A WOKE FUTURE

Some have seen the strength of the anti-woke pushback as a testament to the progress of the progressive movement and its impact on systemic change in America but admit that it may have been too rapid to be embraced by all conservatives. Alternatively, it may indicate that progressive activists have been complacent about previous successes and should strengthen their anti-racism and gender equality positions.

WHAT NEXT FOR WOKE?

The future of woke culture and ideology in society is difficult to predict, as it is a complex and evolving phenomenon. While Wokeism has attracted much attention recently, it is not a new concept. Social justice movements have flourished for decades, even though the benefits and impact on society are an ongoing debate.

Although many conservatives and anti-woke supporters will disagree, political analysts assess that the "culture wars" on woke will not significantly impact Wokeism and that Republicans should be cautious of embracing the anti-woke rhetoric.

The non-partisan research institute NORC and the Wall Street Journal partnered to survey Americans on several hot-button issues relating to "wokeness." They found that most Americans believe progress toward inclusion and diversity is on the right track (Robinson, 2023).

EMBRACING CHANGE

A 2022 global survey showed that people generally embrace change. Across 19 nations surveyed, most people, including Americans (63%), say their country will be better off if it is open to changes (Wike, 2023). However, the gap between the ideological left and right is significantly more in the United States than in other countries, with the Liberals (91%) more likely, than the Conservatives (28%) to believe they will be better off (Wike, 2023). Most agree that the rise of woke culture represents a positive shift towards greater social consciousness and inclusivity and will continue to drive positive change and social reforms in areas such as racial justice and LGBTQIA+ rights.

Political Reforms

One prominent area woke culture will likely impact is the realm of politics. As younger generations mature and become more politically active and engaged, they will bring their cultural values into the political arena, influencing how and why issues and policies are prioritized and pursued. The rise of woke culture will continue to drive increased political activism, to demand systemic change and accountability.

Workplace Reforms

Workplace reforms will continue to reflect the impact of Wokeism. As more companies prioritize DEI initiatives, businesses will respond to pressure to incorporate woke values into their company culture and operations. They will also tend to follow the examples set by others. For instance, in 2023, Target created a whole range of LGBTQIA+ positive clothes and products to celebrate Gay Pride month, encouraging people to embrace diverse identities and LGBTQIA+ rights. This move reflects the shift in public acceptance (Sargent, 2023).

Education Reforms

Education will also continue to be impacted by the woke culture, with many more universities and schools improving their diversity and inclusion training programs to help students and staff become more aware of social justice issues and better equipped to navigate conversations around them even if they have to navigate the issue of race-conscious selection processes within a new legal framework.

Evolving Language

Woke culture will continue to shape our language and the way we talk about social justice issues, with terms like "cisgender," "intersectionality," and "microaggressions" becoming more common as people seek to be more inclusive and sensitive to marginalized groups. In addition, the increased representation of BIPOC and LGBTQIA+ groups in the arts, television, streaming services, and movies contributes to diversifying American culture.

Rebranding Woke

The woke that young activists spoke about in 2012 was idealistic, nuanced, optimistic, and Utopian. And perhaps, at some point, that will become a reality. But in the meantime, Woke as a brand name has lost its shine, and cancel culture and political correctness have dampened its popularity.

One social commentator, Deberry, suggests that it was around 2020 that Black people lost ownership of the word "woke" and that it is now a "white people's word" and should be abandoned (Deberry, 2021). Barg adds, "Once conservatives started labeling corporations as 'woke,' progressives smelled a trend and weren't exactly eager to claim the term for themselves either (Barg, 2021)."

As the attempt to demonize woke continues, it may need a rebranding and a new word to represent this progressive movement. Barg supports the view that "a trend doesn't diminish the importance of antiracist work, which is what wokeness ultimately defines" and adds that conservatives or liberals need to wake up if they think Wokeism is a trend (Barg, 2021). The direction Woke takes next is uncertain, but the viral nature of social media will inevitably give birth to another buzzword or catchy label for social justice activism.

BRIDGING THE WOKE DIVIDE

Communicating effectively with others is the best way to address problems in a polarized political environment. Despite different political leanings, being the model for healthy debate and resolving conflict non-confrontationally can be a powerful influence for those impacted emotionally and psychologically by a toxic culture.

Finding Common Ground

Despite their differences, there are common areas of agreement between Left and Right ideologies. For example, both woke and "anti-woke" proponents may agree on the importance of promoting free speech, critical thinking, and open debate in society and that censorship and silencing of opposing viewpoints harm society.

They may also share the goal of creating a more just and equitable society. However, they may differ on the best means of achieving this goal. Moreover, both woke and "anti-woke" ideologies may agree on the importance of understanding history and context to promote empathy and compassion towards marginalized groups. They may also agree on the need to address issues of inequality and discrimination in society; however, they may differ on the extent and nature of these issues.

One possible way to bridge the divide between these positions is to focus on the common ground and engage in respectful and constructive dialogue. It can involve acknowledging and respecting different perspectives, actively listening, and seeking to understand rather than dismissing opposing viewpoints.

A great example of two politically opposed journalists engaging in respectful debate was documented by Stephen Humphries. Despite a simmering Twitter war between Conor Friedersdorf and Issac Bailey, they never resorted to the anger or vilification that typifies social media debate today. In a 90-minute face-to-face conversation, Humphries describes how they demonstrated it is possible to have thoughtful, respectful interaction and that "taking time to recognize the humanity of the person on the other side matters (Humphries, 2021)."

In their book *Predisposed,* Social Scientists John Hibbing, Kevin Smith, and John Alford, pioneers in biopolitics, suggest that our propensity for being more liberal or conservative may be genetic. Their research shows people with different personality traits favor specific ways of rationalizing and dealing with threats, including political and societal fears. They suggest opposing views can be constructive or destructive, and the fundamental principles of democracy, fairness, and compromise have helped societies navigate high conflict with resounding success. They propose that current bi-partisan viewpoints are healthy in a democratic society and, if handled constructively, can lead to a better nation (Hibbing et al., 2014).

Others suggest that in a society where higher levels of education and affluence are linked, progressive attitudes and policies thrive, with abundant resources to invest in social welfare programs, education, healthcare, and environmental protection. For example, a study by the World Values Survey found that people with higher levels of education were more likely to support gender equality and same-sex marriage, translating into more equitable social policies.

However, the relationship between affluence and progressiveness is not always straightforward. In particular, the United States, one of the wealthiest countries in the world, has one of the highest levels of income inequality, which can be a barrier to adopting progressive policies (Inglehart, 2018). For example, wealthy individuals and corporations may have more significant influence to impede social reform policy decisions on universal healthcare or environmental protection. These are several areas in which Wokeism works to continue positively impacting society.

SUPPORTING WOKEISM

For those who have discovered they align with Wokeism and value the principles of social justice or wish to support others in their lives that are Woke, there are many ways to do so:

Education and Awareness

One of the obstacles to finding common ground is ignorance, which leads to prejudices that create divisions that divide people and cultures. Knowledge and understanding are one way to dismantle those walls and bridge these differences.

Woke platforms can bring public awareness about vital issues of the day, especially concerning political and social injustice. Naia Toke stresses in her 2022 article on Wokeism that it is crucial to continue the research and advocacy about things that matter to people who are oppressed, marginalized, and discriminated against. There are many ways to support activists (Toke, 2022).

Building Relationships

Participating in open discussions shows a willingness to ally with progressive people or groups. Understanding what people are advocating for and why helps build better relationships. This doesn't mean just sympathizing with a cause but engaging in strategies that support social justice and equality (Toke, 2022).

Helping Them to Organize

Many social justice activists have great passion but may lack the skills to organize events or resources. One way to support is by contributing skills or donating money to organizing events.

Help Resolve Conflict and Differences

Separate groups within the Woke Movement may have different goals or objectives. Facilitating dialogue between groups can contribute to resolving conflicts early and prevent groups from undermining each other.

Help Them In Building Communities

Many groups fighting for social justice are based on shared attributes: age, attitudes, beliefs, gender identity, ethnicity, or political leanings. These groups often exist in virtual spaces or are dispersed throughout the community. One way to support them is to help strengthen their communities. Even if someone is not "one of the group," understanding the culture, being sensitive to its needs, and amplifying their voices will all contribute (Toke, 2022).

There are also many small ways that people can help promote equity, diversity, and tolerance. For instance, they can diversify their bookshelves, follow more people of color on social media, support minority-owned businesses, or donate to charitable groups.

TIPS FOR DISCUSSING 'HOT' TOPICS

Most people have had times when they've debated or argued with people when discussing "hot topics." Some communication strategies can help conversations to run smoothly:

- Don't let evidence control the discussion. Many factors influence a person's viewpoint, including past trauma, cultural experience, or exposure to current social media.
- Pointing out random facts will not promote empathy or further discussion. A person's 'truth' depends on values, context, and beliefs.
- It's okay to admit you don't have all the answers or know everything.
- *Listen actively* to what the other person is saying. Keep an open mind and an open ear.

- You don't have to disagree with *everything* they say even though they have opposing views and beliefs or belong to an opposing team.
- Don't take things too personally. Address the idea or opinion, don't attack the person.

Engaging With Young Adults

There are also many ways to support young adults as they navigate the woke world:

- Listen actively and validate their experiences and perspectives.
- Create a safe space for them to express their thoughts and feelings without judgment or criticism.
- Learn more about the issues that matter to them and the language they use to discuss them. It can help better understand their perspective and engage in more meaningful conversations.
- Respect their autonomy and agency. Recognize that young adults can make decisions and take responsibility for their actions.
- Avoid dismissing or minimizing their concerns. Even if there is disagreement with their views, it is essential to acknowledge and respect their right to hold those views.
- Engage in dialogue and debate respectfully and constructively. It can help better understand each other's perspectives and find common ground.
- Be informed about the history and context of social justice issues to better understand the root causes of the problems and provide a basis for constructive discussions.

- Be open-minded and willing to learn from them. Young adults can bring new ideas and perspectives; everyone can benefit from their insights and knowledge.
- Encourage young adults' activism and allow them to participate in causes they care about. It can help young adults feel empowered and engaged in their communities.
- If they wish to participate in rallies and activities, express your concerns authentically without "catastrophizing" and offer to assist their safe participation with a realistic "risk assessment" and practical "exit strategy."
- Practice active empathy by putting yourself in their shoes and trying to understand their point of view. It can help better connect and strengthen their relationships.
- Set boundaries and establish clear expectations around respectful communication and behavior. It can help prevent conflicts and misunderstandings and create a more positive and supportive environment.

By taking these additional steps, parents, teachers, and carers can foster a more meaningful relationship with Woke young adults and demonstrate their commitment to supporting their beliefs and values. In addition, it can help build a stronger, more supportive, and more inclusive community.

17

CONCLUSION

In the light of a 2022 Pew Research Center survey, pessimistic insights into the future of the United States emerged. The consensus among American adults is that by 2050, the landscape will be marked by a weakened economy, diminished global significance, and exacerbated political division (Daniller, 2023).

American society today is challenged by many political issues, especially the wealth gap between the affluent and the destitute (Daniller, 2023). When Americans reflect on the country's past, the present looks worse by comparison, with a majority saying that life is worse today than 50 years ago because of systemic changes to hierarchical power structures and the rapid spread of social reforms in all areas of society.

Yet, amidst this pessimism, Wokeism persists as a powerful instrument for mobilizing collective action around social justice issues. Progressives continue to champion a spectrum of reforms spanning social, political, and economic realms, all aimed at confronting problems as diverse as racial injustice, gender identity, economic disparity, ecological imperatives, healthcare accessibility, and educational equity.

Although Americans do not always fully understand progressive ideologies, their influence profoundly impacts most. As with any contentious and innovative movement, opportunities are present, improvements are possible, and challenges are inevitable. Exploring the different viewpoints that drive debate can yield a deeper understanding of the issues and discourse concerning ongoing social justice issues and the role of woke activism.

This guide has aspired to decipher and demystify some of the complexities and nuances of Woke Culture and explain the concepts associated with Wokeism in today's society.

REFERENCES

AAUP. (2006). *1940 Statement of Principles on Academic Freedom and Tenure*. Academic Association of University Professors. https://www.aaup.org/report/1940-statement-principles-academic-freedom-and-tenure

AAUP. (2007). *Freedom in the Classroom*. Academic Association of University Professors. https://www.aaup.org/report/freedom-classroom

AAUP. (2012). *Freedom and Responsibility*. https://www.aaup.org/report/freedom-and-responsibility

Adams, M., & Bell, L. A. (2016). *Teaching for Diversity and Social Justice*. Routledge. https://philpapers.org/rec/ADATFD

Ahmed, S. (2012). *On being included: Racism and diversity in institutional life*. Duke University Press.

Akomolafe, F. (2021). Decolonizing the Curriculum. In A. Keene, C. O. Minor, & G. Leibowitz (Ed.), *The Palgrave Handbook of Race and Ethnic Inequalities in Education* (pp. 477–496). Springer.

Alphonse, L. (2019). The Impact Generation: How Gen Z Is Using Social Media for Good. *Forbes*. Advance online publication. https://doi.org/Media

Altschuler, G. C., & Wippman, D. (2023, September 4). The myth of 'woke' indoctrination of students. *The Hill*. https://thehill.com/opinion/education/3941143-the-myth-of-woke-indoctrination-of-students/

America Succeeds. (2022). *Advancing Equity in Education*. America Succeeds. https://americasucceeds.org/policy-priorities/equity-in-education

Amnesty. (2020). *'I can't breathe': The refrain that reignited a movement*. Amnesty International. https://www.amnesty.org/en/latest/news/2020/06/i-cant-breathe-refrain-reignited-movement/

Anderson, K., Taylor, M., Ramachandra, P., & Wynnychenko, R. (2021). *Analyzing Representation in the United States Congress*. Common Cause Illinois. https://www.commoncause.org/illinois/democracy-wire/analyzing-representation-in-the-united-states-congress/

Angus, H. (2019, March 21). Cancel Culture: Moral Panic or Reality? *Medium*. https://haaniyah.medium.com/cancel-culture-moral-panic-or-reality-7eeb1f3c1242

The Athletic (2021, May 3). LeBron James, More Than A Vote to launch campaign during NBA All-Star weekend. *The Athletic*. https://theathletic.com/4222791/2021/03/04/lebron-james-more-than-a-vote-to-launch-campaign-during-nba-all-star-weekend/

Atske, S., & Vogels, E. A. (2021). *Americans and 'Cancel Culture': Where Some See Calls for Accountability, Others See Censorship, Punishment*. https://www.pewre

search.org/internet/2021/05/19/americans-and-cancel-culture-where-some-see-calls-for-accountability-others-see-censorship-punishment/

Auld, G., & Grabs, J. (2022, October 6). *Has Patagonia defined a new gold standard for business responsibility?* https://theconversation.com/has-patagonia-defined-a-new-gold-standard-for-business-responsibility-191250

Ayala, R. (2021). *Community-Led Clean Energy Strategies.* American Council for Energy Efficient Economy. https://storymaps.arcgis.com/stories/88cd8a715089418890d9ec4d09a25648

Barg, J. (2020, September 7). How 'cancel culture' caught on so quickly. *The Philadelphia Inquirer.* https://www.inquirer.com/opinion/cancel-culture-language-linguistics-grammar-20200708.html

Barg, J. (2021, May 8). How the right stole 'woke' and turned it into a derisive insult | The Angry Grammarian. *The Philadelphia Inquirer.* https://www.inquirer.com/opinion/woke-bill-maher-olympics-republicans-right-language-20210804.html

Barrett, J. (2021). *Anti-woke campaigners take aim at pronouns.* www.bbc.com/news/uk-politics-5696881

BE Initiative. (2023). *Community-owned renewable energy projects – Black Environmental Initiative.* Black Environmental Initiative. https://beinitiative.com/community-owned-green-projects/

Beckham, B. (2017). *Garvey Lives.* Beckham Publication Group. My Book

Black, H. A. (2023). *The Dumbing Down of American Education.* The Knoxville Focus. https://www.knoxfocus.com/archives/this-weeks-focus/the-dumbing-down-of-american-education/

BLM. (2019). *Herstory.* Black Lives Matter. https://blacklivesmatter.com/herstory/

Borysenko, K. (2020, February 13). The Dark Side Of #MeToo: What Happens When Men Are Falsely Accused. *Forbes.* https://www.forbes.com/sites/karlynborysenko/2020/02/12/the-dark-side-of-metoo-what-happens-when-men-are-falsely-accused/?sh=d2abc8b864d8

Bower, T. (2019). *The #MeToo Backlash.* Harvard Business Review. https://hbr.org/2019/09/the-metoo-backlash

Bowman, B. (2023, April 27). 'A country on fire': New poll finds America polarized over culture, race and 'woke'. *NBC News.* https://www.nbcnews.com/meet-the-press/first-read/-country-fire-new-poll-finds-america-polarized-culture-race-woke-rcna81592

Britannica. (2023). *Abolitionism.* Brittanica. https://www.britannica.com/topic/abolitionism-European-and-American-social-movement/Southern-defense-of-the-peculiar-institution

Brito, C. (2020, August 20). "Cancel culture" seems to have started as an internet joke. Now it's anything but. *CBS News.* https://www.cbsnews.com/news/cancel-culture-internet-joke-anything-but/

Brockes, E. (2018, January 15). #MeToo founder Tarana Burke: 'You have to use your privilege to serve other people'. *The Guardian*. https://www.theguardian.com/world/2018/jan/15/me-too-founder-tarana-burke-women-sexual-assault

Broderick, R., Nigatu, H., & Testa, J. (2014). *What Is Rape Culture?* Buzzfeednews. https://www.buzzfeednews.com/article/ryanhatesthis/what-is-rape-culture

Brown-Jeffy, S., & Cooper, J. E. (2011). Toward a Conceptual Framework of Culturally Relevant Pedagogy: An Overview of the Conceptual and Theoretical Literature. *Teacher Education Quarterly, Winter*.

Brubaker, R. (2020, October 9). The Danger of Race Reductionism. *Persuasion*. https://www.persuasion.community/p/the-danger-of-race-reductionism

Bullard Centre. (2023). *The Bullard Center.* The Bullard Center For Environmental Justice. https://www.bullardcenter.org/

Cammaerts, B. (2022). The abnormalisation of social justice: The 'anti-woke culture war' discourse in the UK. *Discourse & Society, 33*(6), 730–743. https://doi.org/10.1177/09579265221095407

Campbell, B., & Manning, J. (2018). *The Rise of Victimhood Culture: Microaggressions, Safe Spaces, and the New Culture Wars.* Macmillan.

Cauley, K. (2019). *Word: Woke*. Believer Magazine. https://www.thebeliever.net/kashana-cauley-word-woke/?preview=true

CBS News. (2020a). *Speaking Frankly: Censorship*. CBS News. https://www.cbsnews.com/video/cbs-reports-presents-speaking-frankly-censorship/

CBS News (2020b, August 13). Speaking Frankly: Cancel Culture. *CBS News*. https://www.cbsnews.com/video/cbs-reports-presents-speaking-frankly-cancel-culture/

CBS News. (2021). *The Diversity Dilemma*. CBS News. https://www.cbsnews.com/video/cbs-reports-the-diversity-dilemma/

The Center. (2023). *Defining LGBTQIA+*. The Lesbian, Gay, Bisexual & Transgender Community Center. https://gaycenter.org/about/lgbtq/

CEP. (2020). *History and Evolution of Public Education in the US*. Center on Education Policy.

Cherry, K. (2022). *What Does LGBTQ+ Mean?* Very Well Mind. https://www.verywellmind.com/what-does-lgbtq-mean-5069804

Choi, A. (2023). *Record number of anti-LGBTQ bills have been introduced this year | CNN Politics*. https://edition.cnn.com/2023/04/06/politics/anti-lgbtq-plus-state-bill-rights-dg/index.html

Chotiner, I. (2021, July 15). Robin DiAngelo Wants White Progressives to Look Inward. *The New Yorker*. https://www.newyorker.com/news/q-and-a/robin-diangelo-wants-white-progressives-to-look-inward

Clancy, L. (2023, June 2). *Americans differ by party, ideology over the impact of social media on U.S. democracy*. https://www.pewresearch.org/short-reads/2022/12/14/americans-differ-by-party-ideology-over-the-impact-of-social-media-on-u-s-democracy/

Climate Justice Alliance. (2023). *Just Transition*. Climate Justice Alliance. https://climatejusticealliance.org/just-transition/

CNN. (2019). *Conservative journalist Andy Ngo says Antifa attacked him in Portland | CNN*. https://edition.cnn.com/videos/us/2019/07/02/antifa-conservative-journalist-andy-ngo-bts-newday-vpx.cnn

Cohen, S [Seth] (2020, May 31). 'For Once, Don't Do It': The Powerful Idea Behind Nike's New Anti-Racism Ad. *Forbes*. https://www.forbes.com/sites/sethcohen/2020/05/30/for-once-dont-do-it---the-powerful-idea-behind-nikes-new-anti-racism-ad/?sh=66c81eba2fdb

Cohen, S [Stanley]. (2002). *Folk Devils and Moral Panics: The Creation of Mods and Rockers*. Routledge.

Cohn, N. (2023, March 24). What's 'Woke' and Why It Matters. *The New York Times*. https://www.nytimes.com/2023/03/24/upshot/woke-meaning-democrats-republicans.html

Cone, S., Gold, K., Harris, A., & Ladak, S. (2022). *Workplace Conduct Still Needs Improvement After #MeToo*. Bloomberg Law. https://news.bloomberglaw.com/daily-labor-report/workplace-conduct-still-needs-improvement-after-metoo

Contreras, J. (2023, May 2). DeSantis ramps up 'war on woke' with new attacks on Florida higher education. *The Guardian*. https://www.theguardian.com/us-news/2023/feb/05/ron-desantis-war-on-woke-florida-higher-education-new-college

Cooperman, A. (2023, May 11). *Most U.S. parents pass along their religion and politics to their children*. https://www.pewresearch.org/short-reads/2023/05/10/most-us-parents-pass-along-their-religion-and-politics-to-their-children/

Copeland, T. (2021, March 8). Oppression Olympics: The Game That Needs to End. *Central Indiana Community Foundation*. https://www.cicf.org/2021/08/02/oppression-olympics-the-game-that-needs-to-end/

Crawford, G. (2022, June 28). Fostering Diversity In Higher Education To Power Creativity. *Forbes*. https://www.forbes.com/sites/forbesbusinesscouncil/2022/06/28/fostering-diversity-in-higher-education-to-power-creativity/?sh=66db341e35e4

Crenshaw, K. (1989). *Demarginalizing the intersection of race and sex: A black feminist critique of antidiscrimination doctrine, feminist theory and antiracist politics*. University of Chicago Legal Forum.

Daniller, A. (2023, April 25). *Americans take a dim view of the nation's future, look more positively at the past*. https://www.pewresearch.org/short-reads/2023/04/24/americans-take-a-dim-view-of-the-nations-future-look-more-positively-at-the-past/

Dart, T. (2016, August 12). White nationalist Richard Spencer fuels protest as he mocks critics in Texas. *The Guardian*. https://www.theguardian.com/us-news/2016/dec/07/white-nationalist-richard-spencer-texas-am

Deberry, J. (2021). *Opinion | White people have twisted the definition of 'woke' beyond recognition*. https://www.msnbc.com/opinion/woke-has-been-weaponized-label-those-fighting-oppression-oppressors-n1284129

Del Pilar, W. (2023). *A Brief History of Affirmative Action and the Assault on Race-Conscious Admissions*. Education Trust. https://edtrust.org/

Delao, M. (2021). *A Brief Look at the Four Waves of Feminism* -. TheHumanist.com. https://thehumanist.com/commentary/a-brief-look-at-the-four-waves-of-feminism/

Delgado, R., & Stefancic, J. (2017). *Critical Race Theory: An Introduction* (4th). New York University Press. https://nyupress.org/9781479818259/critical-race-theory-fourth-edition/

Denning, S. (2020). *Why Stakeholder Capitalism Will Fail*. Forbes. https://www.forbes.com/sites/stevedenning/2020/01/05/why-stakeholder-capitalism-will-fail/?sh=78d4ef03785a

DiAngelo, R. (2018). *White Fragility: Why It's So Hard For White People To Talk About Racism*. Beacon Press.

Doyle, A. (2022, February 3). The liberal case against pronouns. *UnHerd*. https://unherd.com/2022/03/the-liberal-case-against-pronouns/

Dreier, P. (2018). *The #MeToo Movement's Roots in Women Workers' Rights*. Common Dreams. https://www.commondreams.org/views/2018/10/14/metoo-move ments-roots-women-workers-rights

D'souza, D. (2022). *Understanding Stakeholder Capitalism, Its History, and Relevance*. Investopedia. https://www.investopedia.com/stakeholder-capitalism-4774323

Edesess, M. (2021). *How Bad is "Woke" Capitalism?* Advisor Perspectives. https://www.advisorperspectives.com/articles/2021/09/13/how-bad-is-woke-capitalism

Ekins, E. (2020). *Poll: 62% of Americans say they have political views they're afraid to share*. The Village News. https://www.villagenews.com/story/2020/08/06/opinion/poll-62-of-americans-say-they-have-political-views-theyre-afraid-to-share/62817.html

Ellis, N. T. (2023, June 30). The gutting of affirmative action is a 'clear and present danger' to equal education, critics say. *CNN*. https://edition.cnn.com/2023/06/29/us/affirmative-action-impact-reaj/index.html

Erickson-Schroth, L., & Davis, B. (2021). *Gender: What everyone needs to know. What Everyone Needs to Know Ser*. Oxford University Press; ProQuest. https://ebookcentral.proquest.com/lib/kxp/detail.action?docID=6403000

Fight for $15. (2023, June 6). *Fight for $15*. https://fightfor15.org/

FOEI. (2023). *Climate litigation - for social and environmental justice*. Friends of the Earth International. https://www.foei.org/what-we-do/climate-justice-and-energy/climate-litigation/

Foucart, S. (2022, December 7). 'Environmentalism is, to a large extent, a kind of 'wokeism''. *Le Monde*. https://www.lemonde.fr/en/opinion/article/2022/

07/11/environmentalism-is-to-a-large-extent-a-kind-of-wokeism_5989800_23.html

Fridays For Future. (2021). *How Greta started a global movement.* Fridays For Future. https://fridaysforfuture.org/what-we-do/who-we-are/

Friedersdorf, C. (2015, November 9). Microaggressions and the Rise of Victimhood Culture. *The Atlantic.* https://www.theatlantic.com/politics/archive/2015/09/the-rise-of-victimhood-culture/404794/

Friedman, M. (1970, September 13). A Friedman doctrine-- The Social Responsibility Of Business Is to Increase Its Profits. *The New York Times.* https://www.nytimes.com/1970/09/13/archives/a-friedman-doctrine-the-social-responsi bility-of-business-is-to.html

Gay, R. (2021, July 17). Why People Are So Awful Online. *The New York Times.* https://www.nytimes.com/2021/07/17/opinion/culture/social-media-cancel-culture-roxane-gay.html

Geiger, A., & Davis, L. (2019, December 7). A growing number of American teenagers – particularly girls – are facing depression. *Pew Research Center.* https://www.pewresearch.org/fact-tank/2019/07/12/a-growing-number-of-american-teenagers-particularly-girls-are-facing-depression/

GLAAD (2023, February 6). Accelerating Acceptance 2023. *GLAAD.* https://glaad.org/publications/accelerating-acceptance-2023/

Gordon, S. (2022). *What Is the #MeToo Movement?* Very Well Mind. https://www.verywellmind.com/what-is-the-metoo-movement-4774817

Grady, C. (2018). *The waves of feminism, and why people keep fighting over them, explained.* Vox. https://www.vox.com/2018/3/20/16955588/feminism-waves-explained-first-second-third-fourth

Graham, D. A. (2023, March 20). Wokeness Has Replaced Socialism as the Great Conservative Bogeyman. *The Atlantic.* https://www.theatlantic.com/ideas/archive/2023/03/wokeness-socialism-liberal-threat-public-discourse/673430/

Grant, L. (Director). (2022). *Stay Woke: The Black Lives Matter Movement.*

Greenpeace. (2022). *A Brief History of Environmentalism - Greenpeace International.* Greenpeace International. https://www.greenpeace.org/international/story/11658/a-brief-history-of-environmentalism/

Greenwood, S., & Wike, R. (2022). *Social Media Seen as Mostly Good for Democracy Across Many Nations, But U.S. is a Major Outlier.* https://www.pewresearch.org/global/2022/12/06/social-media-seen-as-mostly-good-for-democracy-across-many-nations-but-u-s-is-a-major-outlier/#americans-most-likely-to-say-social-media-has-been-bad-for-democracy

Grinspan, J. (2021). The Forgotten Precedent for Our 'Unprecedented' Political Insanity. *Politico.* https://www.politico.com/news/magazine/2021/04/24/forgotten-precedent-unprecedented-politics-age-of-acrimony-484072

Haidt, J. (2022a). *The Polarization Spiral. - NYU Stern.* New York University.

https://www.stern.nyu.edu/experience-stern/faculty-research/the-polarization-spiral

Haidt, J. (2022b). *When Truth and Social Justice Collide, Choose Truth*. The Chronicle of Higher Education. https://www.chronicle.com/article/when-truth-and-social-justice-collide-choose-truth?emailConfirmed=true&supportSignUp=true&supportForgotPassword=true&email=nyxstyx64%40gmail.com&success=true&code=success&bc_nonce=ej1m1q6j44vjfzn1s3b4z&cid=gen_sign_in

Haislop, T. (2020, September 13). Colin Kaepernick kneeling timeline: How protests during the national anthem started a movement in the NFL. https://www.sportingnews.com/us/nfl/news/colin-kaepernick-kneeling-protest-timeline/xktu6ka4diva1s5jxaylrcsse

Hammer, A. (2023). *Activists erupt as Iowa diocese enacts anti-woke rules in schools*. https://www.dailymail.co.uk/news/article-11642739/Activists-erupt-Diocese-Des-Moines-enacts-anti-woke-rules-churches-schools.html

Hampton, R., & Kircher, M. M. (2021, June 23). Hey, White Liberals: You're Using "Woke" Wrong. *Slate*. https://slate.com/culture/2021/06/woke-critical-race-theory-definition-history-meaningless.html

Harmon, B. (2022, March 9). What does 'woke' mean? Is 'woke ideology' anti-American? | Opinion. *Deseret News*. https://www.deseret.com/opinion/2022/9/2/23331757/opinion-meaning-of-woke-awareness-injustice

Harriot, M. (2022, December 21). War on wokeness: the year the right rallied around a made-up menace. *The Guardian*. https://www.theguardian.com/us-news/2022/dec/20/anti-woke-race-america-history

Harvard Graduate School of Education. (2023, July 5). *The Case for Affirmative Action*. https://www.gse.harvard.edu/news/uk/18/07/case-affirmative-action

Hawkins, S., Yudkin, D., Juan-Torres, M., & Dixon, T. (2018). *The Hidden Tribes of America: A Study of America's Polarized Landscape*. More in Common. https://hiddentribes.us/

Henley, J. (2023, July 7). Greta Thunberg charged with disobeying Swedish police during oil protest. *The Guardian*. https://www.theguardian.com/environment/2023/jul/06/greta-thunberg-charged-with-disobeying-swedish-police-during-oil-protest

Hibbing, J. R., Smith, K. B., & Alford, J. R. (2014). *Predisposed: Liberals, conservatives, and the biology of political differences*. Routledge.

Hill, J. (2021, May 29). George Floyd's Murder Forced Athletes to Find Their Voice. *The Atlantic*. https://www.theatlantic.com/ideas/archive/2021/05/george-floyd-murder-athletes-sports-public-life/619043/

Hillman, N. (2020). *Why Rich Colleges Get Richer & Poor Colleges Get Poorer: The Case for Equity-Based Funding in Higher Education – Third Way*. Third Way. https://www.thirdway.org/report/why-rich-colleges-get-richer-poor-colleges-get-poorer-the-case-for-equity-based-funding-in-higher-education

Horowitz, J. M., Hurst, K., & Braga, D. (2023). *Support for the Black Lives Matter*

Movement Has Dropped Considerably From Its Peak in 2020. Pew Research Center. https://www.pewresearch.org/social-trends/2023/06/14/support-for-the-black-lives-matter-movement-has-dropped-considerably-from-its-peak-in-2020/

Housman, P. (2022). *Roe v Wade Overturned: What It Means, What's Next*. American University. https://www.american.edu/cas/news/roe-v-wade-overturned-what-it-means-whats-next.cfm

Human Rights Campaign. (2023). *Equality for All Not for Some*. Human Rights Campaign. https://www.hrc.org/

Humphries, S. (2021). *When a Twitter war gets … respectful?* The Christian Science Moniter. https://www.csmonitor.com/USA/Society/2021/0528/When-a-Twitter-war-gets-respectful

Hurley, B. (2023, September 6). 'Central Park Karen' loses appeal over firing from job. *The Independent*. https://www.independent.co.uk/news/world/americas/central-park-karen-amy-cooper-appeal-b2354202.html

Inglehart, R. (2018). *Cultural evolution: People's motivations are changing, and reshaping the world*. Cambridge University Press. https://doi.org/10.1017/9781108613880

Ingraham, C. (2016). *The dramatic shift among college professors that's hurting students' education*. https://www.washingtonpost.com/news/wonk/wp/2016/01/11/the-dramatic-shift-among-college-professors-thats-hurting-students-education/

Janes, C. (2023). *Top 10 Cancelled Celebrities: Where Are They Now? | Articles on WatchMojo.com*. https://www.watchmojo.com/articles/top-10-cancelled-celebrities-where-are-they-now

Jarratt-Snider, K., & Nielsen, M. O. (Eds.). (2020). *Indigenous justice. Indigenous environmental justice*. The University of Arizona Press. https://www.jstor.org/stable/10.2307/j.ctv10qqwrm

Jerkins, M. (2019, October 15). Tarana Burke on the way forward for MeToo. *Vox*. https://www.vox.com/identities/2019/10/15/20910298/tarana-burke-morgan-jerkins

Jones, J. M. (2023, February 22). U.S. LGBT Identification Steady at 7.2%. *Gallup*. https://news.gallup.com/poll/470708/lgbt-identification-steady.aspx

Justas. (2022). *Critical Pedagogy: 8 key concepts you need to know*. https://www.dns-tvind.dk/critical-pedagogy/

Kalin, M., & Sambanis, N. (2018). How to Think About Social Identity. *Annual Review of Political Science, 21*(1), 239–257. https://doi.org/10.1146/annurev-polisci-042016-024408

Kaplan, S. (2020, June 30). Climate change is also a racial justice problem. *The Washington Post*. https://www.washingtonpost.com/climate-solutions/2020/06/29/climate-change-racism/

Kelley, W. M. (1962, May 20). If You're Woke You Dig It; No mickey mouse can be expected to follow today's Negro idiom without a hip assist. If You're

Woke You Dig It. *The New York Times*. https://www.nytimes.com/1962/05/20/archives/if-youre-woke-you-dig-it-no-mickey-mouse-can-be-expected-to-follow.html?legacy=true

Kendi, I. X. (2019). *How to be an anti-Racist*. One World.

Khalid, A., & Snyder, J. (2022, June 10). Interview by H. Muncy.

Khazan, O. (2021a, September 27). Counterweight and the Movement Against Wokeness. *The Atlantic*. https://www.theatlantic.com/politics/archive/2021/09/counterweight-cancel-culture-support-ground/620203/

Khazan, O. (2021b, December 11). Young People, Not College Grads, Drive Wokeness. *The Atlantic*. https://www.theatlantic.com/politics/archive/2021/11/young-people-college-grads-wokeness/620674/

Klawe, M. (2019, January 5). Why We Need Inclusive Teaching In Every Classroom. *Forbes*. https://www.forbes.com/sites/mariaklawe/2019/04/30/why-we-need-inclusive-teaching-in-every-classroom/?sh=21196a5a2d61

Knowles, H. (2023, April 17). You asked: Why are Republicans so focused on 'wokeness'? *The Washington Post*. https://www.washingtonpost.com/politics/2023/04/17/republican-wokeness-gop-primary/

Kober, N. (2020a). *For the Common Good: Recommiting to Public Education in a Time of Crisis*. Center on Education Policy. https://www.cep-dc.org/

Kober, N. (2020b). *History and Evolution of Public Education in the US*. Center on Education Policy. https://www.cep-dc.org/

Labaree, D. F. (2010). *Someone Has to Fail_ The Zero-Sum Game of Public Schooling*. Harvard University Press. https://www.academia.edu/37144927/Someone_Has_to_Fail_The_Zero_Sum_Game_of_Public_Schooling_Harvard_University_Press_2010_pdf

Levine, I. (2022, May 24). Woke Capitalism's Tragedy of the Commons. *Quillette*. https://quillette.com/2022/05/24/woke-capitalisms-tragedy-of-the-commons/

Lewis, H. (2020a, July 14). Cancel Culture and the Problem of Woke Capitalism. *The Atlantic*. https://www.theatlantic.com/international/archive/2020/07/cancel-culture-and-problem-woke-capitalism/614086/

Lewis, H. (2020b, October 27). The World Is Trapped in America's Culture War. *The Atlantic*. https://www.theatlantic.com/international/archive/2020/10/internet-world-trapped-americas-culture-war/616799/

Lewis, P. (2017). *'I see things differently': James Damore on his autism and the Google memo*. The Guardian. https://www.theguardian.com/technology/2017/nov/16/james-damore-google-memo-interview-autism-regrets

Lindsay, J. (2020, July 6). The Cult Dynamics of Wokeness. *New Discourses*. https://newdiscourses.com/2020/06/cult-dynamics-wokeness/

Linker, D. (2021, March 16). What the woke revolution is — and isn't. *The Week*. https://theweek.com/articles/972066/what-woke-revolution--isnt

Liu, R. (2020). *#Woke: The Dangers and Possibilities of Social Media Activism and Woke Washing*. Impakter. https://impakter.com/woke-the-dangers-and-possibilities-of-social-media-activism-and-woke-washing/

Livingston, M. (2020, June 16). These are the major brands donating to the Black Lives Matter movement. *CNET*. https://www.cnet.com/culture/companies-donating-black-lives-matter/

Livingstone, R. (2020). *How to Promote Racial Equity in the Workplace*. Harvard Review. https://hbr.org/2020/09/how-to-promote-racial-equity-in-the-workplace

Lombroso, D. (2020, November 6). White Noise: A Documentary on the Rise of the Alt-Right. *The Atlantic*. https://www.theatlantic.com/politics/archive/2020/06/white-noise-documentary-alt-right/612898/

Losen, D. J., & Martinez, T. E. (2013). *Out of School and Off Track: The Overuse of Suspensions in American Middle and High Schools The Civil Rights Project at UCLA*. UCLA. https://civilrightsproject.ucla.edu/resources/projects/center-for-civil-rights-remedies/school-to-prison-folder/federal-reports/out-of-school-and-off-track-the-overuse-of-suspensions-in-american-middle-and-high-schools

Luk, J. (2021, June 24). Why 'woke' became toxic. *Al Jazeera*. https://www.aljazeera.com/opinions/2021/6/24/what-is-woke-culture-and-why-has-it-become-so-toxic

Lyons, N. S. (2023). *The Woke Revolution is Far from Over – Quadrant Online*. Quadrant. https://quadrant.org.au/magazine/2023/01/the-woke-revolution-is-far-from-over/

Mandelaro, J. (2021). *Ibram X. Kendi: 'The very heartbeat of racism is denial'*. University of Rochester. https://www.rochester.edu/newscenter/ibram-x-kendi-the-very-heartbeat-of-racism-is-denial-470332/

Mandelbaum, M. (2020). *Political Correctness Threatens American Higher Education - The American Interest*. The American Interest. https://www.the-american-interest.com/2020/02/28/political-correctness-threatens-american-higher-education/

Manhattan Institute. (2021). *Woke Schooling: A Toolkit for Concerned Parents | Manhattan Institute*. Manhattan Institute. https://www.manhattan-institute.org/woke-schooling-toolkit-for-concerned-parents

Mathis, S., & Stedman, C. (2023). *What is environmental, social and governance (ESG)?* Tech Target. https://www.techtarget.com/whatis/definition/environmental-social-and-governance-ESG

Mclennan, D., & Whitney, R. M. (2022). *Why Generation Z might not be as 'woke' as most think*. The Hill. https://thehill.com/opinion/congress-blog/3682216-why-generation-z-might-not-be-as-woke-as-most-think/

McWhorter, J. (2021a). *The Elect: The Threat to a Progressive America From Anti-black Anti-racists*. It Bears Mentioning. https://johnmcwhorter.substack.com/p/the-elect-the-threat-to-a-progressive

McWhorter, J. (2021b). *Woke racism: How a new religion has betrayed Black America*. Portfolio/Penguin.

Mendenhall, A. (2022, September 15). Corporate Wokeness Hurts the Groups It

Purports to Help. https://www.aier.org/article/corporate-wokeness-hurts-the-groups-it-purports-to-help/

Merriam-Webster. (2022, October 22). *Definition of WOKE*. https://www.merriam-webster.com/dictionary/woke

Miles-Hercules, D., & Muwwakkil, J. (2021). Virtue Signaling and the Linguistic Repertoire of Anti-Blackness: Or, "I Would Have Voted for Obama for a Third Term". *Journal of Linguistic Anthropology, 31*(2), 267–270. https://doi.org/10.1111/jola.12320

Milk Foundation. (2023). *The Official Harvey Milk Biography –*. Harvey Milk Foundation. https://milkfoundation.org/about/harvey-milk-biography

Minkin, R. (2023). *Diversity, Equity and Inclusion in the Workplace*. Pew Research Center. https://www.pewresearch.org/social-trends/2023/05/17/diversity-equity-and-inclusion-in-the-workplace/

Mitchell, T., & Parker, K. (2019). *The Growing Partisan Divide in Views of Higher Education*. https://www.pewresearch.org/social-trends/2019/08/19/the-growing-partisan-divide-in-views-of-higher-education-2/

Morris, B. J. (2009, October 22). *A brief history of lesbian, gay, bisexual, and transgender social movements*. https://www.apa.org/topics/lgbtq/history

Moses, W. J. (2020). Global Garveyism. *Journal of American History, 107*(1), 237–238. https://doi.org/10.1093/jahist/jaaa119

Mosier, C. (2022, June 29). As elite sports think again about trans participation, our only demand is for fairness. *The Guardian*. https://www.theguardian.com/commentisfree/2022/jun/29/sports-trans-participation-transgender-women-swimming

MTM. (2023). *Me Too Movement*. Me Too Movement. https://metoomvmt.org/

Multiview. (2021). *Stakeholder Capitalism vs Shareholder Capitalism*. Multiview Corporation. https://multiviewcorp.com/blog/stakeholder-vs-shareholder-capitalism-are-we-at-a-pivotal-moment

Murawski, J. (2019, September 18). Woke history is making big inroads in America's high schools. *The Spectator World*. https://thespectator.com/topic/woke-history-inroads-america-high-schools/

Nadeem, R. (2021a). *11. Progressive Left*. https://www.pewresearch.org/politics/2021/11/09/progressive-left/

Nadeem, R. (2021b). *13. How the political typology groups view major issues*. https://www.pewresearch.org/politics/2021/11/09/how-the-political-typology-groups-view-major-issues/

Nadeem, R. (2021c). *3. Faith and Flag Conservatives*. https://www.pewresearch.org/politics/2021/11/09/faith-and-flag-conservatives/

Nadeem, R. (2021d). *8. Outsider Left*. https://www.pewresearch.org/politics/2021/11/09/outsider-left/

Nadeem, R., & Tyson, A. (2021). *Gen Z, Millennials Stand Out for Climate Change Activism, Social Media Engagement With Issue*. https://www.pewresearch.org/

science/2021/05/26/gen-z-millennials-stand-out-for-climate-change-activism-social-media-engagement-with-issue/

NEA. (2021). *Racial Justice in Education Framework.* National Education Association. https://www.nea.org/resource-library/racial-justice-education-framework

NFL. (2022). *Inspire Change - NFL Social Justice Initiative.* NFL. https://www.nfl.com/causes/inspire-change/resources/support-for-social-justice

NMAAHC. (2021). *The Foundations of Black Power.* National Museum of African American History and Culture. https://nmaahc.si.edu/explore/stories/foundations-black-power

NPS. (2023). *John Muir.* National Park Service. https://www.nps.gov/articles/john-muir.htm

NRDC. (2023). *Indigenous Leaders at the Frontlines of Environmental Injustice and Solutions.* National Resources Defense Council. https://www.nrdc.org/bio/giulia-cs-good-stefani/indigenous-leaders-frontlines-environmental-injustice-and-solutions

NWLC. (2022). *Fifteen States Have Passed New Laws Protecting Workers from Sexual Harassment in Wake of #MeToo, NWLC Report Reveals - National Women's Law Center.* National Women's Law Center. https://nwlc.org/press-release/fifteen-states-have-passed-new-laws-protecting-workers-from-sexual-harassment-in-wake-of-metoo-nwlc-report-reveals/

NWPC. (2023). *About - National Women's Political Caucus.* National Women's Political Caucus. https://www.nwpc.org/about/

Ogrysko, N. (2021, June 29). Biden creates sweeping diversity and inclusion initiative through new executive order. *Federal News Network.* https://federalnewsnetwork.com/workforce/2021/06/biden-creates-sweeping-diversity-and-inclusion-initiative-through-new-executive-order/

O'Neil, C., & Baker, S. (2022). *The shame machine: Who profits in the new age of humiliation* (First edition). Crown.

Pappas, S. (2012, May 28). Political Polarization 'Dangerous,' Psychologist Says. *Live Science.* https://www.livescience.com/20609-political-polarization-dangerous-psychology.html

Parker, K., Graf, N., & Igielnik, R. (2019). *Generation Z Looks a Lot Like Millennials on Key Social and Political Issues.* Pew Research Centre. https://www.pewresearch.org/social-trends/2019/01/17/generation-z-looks-a-lot-like-millennials-on-key-social-and-political-issues/

PBS. (2014). *Timeline of Environmental Movement and History.* PBS. American Masters. https://www.pbs.org/wnet/americanmasters/a-fierce-green-fire-timeline-of-environmental-movement/2988/

Pender Greene, M. (2022). *Oppression Olympics - Undoing Racism Resources.* https://marypendergreene.com/bookshelf/oppression-olympics/

Pierce, S. (2023, March 4). 2024 election: Is wokeness a losing issue for DeSantis, GOP? | Opinion. *Deseret News.* https://www.deseret.com/2023/4/2/

23641903/ron-desantis-florida-wokeness-politics-gop-2024-election?utm_source=twitter&utm_medium=dn-social&utm_campaign=twitter&utm_content=deseretnews

Pinker, S. (2018). *Enlightenment now: The case for reason, science, humanism, and progress*. Viking an imprint of Penguin Random House LLC.

Powell, J. A., & Menedian, S. (2017). *The Problem of Othering: Towards Inclusiveness and Belonging - Othering and Belonging*. Othering and Belonging.Org. https://www.otheringandbelonging.org/the-problem-of-othering/

Prest, M. (2020, December 8). NBA Commits $300 Million for Economic Development in Black Communities (Grants Roundup). *The Chronicle of Philanthropy*. https://www.philanthropy.com/article/nba-commits-300-million-for-economic-development-in-black-communities-grants-roundup

Principato, C. (2022, February 8). Future of ESG Investing Unclear Amid Inflation, Regulatory Scrutiny. *Morning Consult*. https://pro.morningconsult.com/analysis/future-of-esg-investing-amid-inflation-regulatory-scrutiny

Pruitt, S. (2022). *What Are the Four Waves of Feminism?* History.com. https://www.history.com/news/feminism-four-waves

Ramaswamy, V. (2021). *Woke, Inc: Inside corporate America's social justice scam* (First edition). Center Street.

Redding, J. (1942). *Negro Digest, 1*.

Roberts, M. (2023, March 20). The right wing's 'woke' obsession could come back to haunt it. *The Washington Post*. https://www.washingtonpost.com/opinions/2023/03/20/svb-woke-insult-history/

Robinson, E. (2023, March 28). 'Wokeness' is winning. *The Washington Post*. https://www.washingtonpost.com/opinions/2023/03/27/woke-values-survey-norc-university-of-chicago/

Rockenbach, A. N., Mayhew, M. J., Singer, K., & Dahl, L. S. (2020, February 3). Professors change few minds on politics—but conservative ones may have more influence. *The Washington Post*. https://www.washingtonpost.com/politics/2020/03/02/conservative-faculty-appear-influence-their-students-more-than-liberal-professors-do/

Rockenbach, A. N., Selznick, B. S., Zagorsky, J. L., & Mayhew, M. J. (2023, May 10). *Does college turn people into liberals?* https://theconversation.com/does-college-turn-people-into-liberals-90905

Romano, A. (2020, October 10). What is woke: How a Black movement watchword got co-opted in a culture war. *Vox*. https://www.vox.com/culture/21437879/stay-woke-wokeness-history-origin-evolution-controversy

Romano, A. (2022, September 17). The Little Mermaid remake: The racist backlash over increased diversity, explained. *Vox*. https://www.vox.com/culture/23357114/the-little-mermaid-racist-backlash-lotr-rings-of-power-diversity-controversy

Rubin, J. (2023, May 6). With an ode to the First Amendment, a judge rebuffs the war on woke. *The Washington Post*. https://www.washingtonpost.com/opinions/2023/06/06/republicans-woke-court/

Rufo, C. F. (2021, July 23). Ibram X. Kendi is the false prophet of a dangerous and lucrative faith. *New York Post*. https://nypost.com/2021/07/22/ibram-x-kendi-is-the-false-prophet-of-a-dangerous-and-lucrative-faith/

Rugy, V. de (2022a, May 25). Corporations' Woke Signaling Won't Override Profit Motive. *Spectator*. https://spectator.org/corporations-woke-signaling-wont-override-profit-motive/

Rugy, V. de (2022b, May 27). 'Woke Capitalism' Does Not Advance Social Justice. *Reason Magazine*. https://reason.com/2022/05/26/woke-capitalism-does-not-advance-social-justice/

Runnels, R. (2018). *Marginalized groups within LGBTQ umbrella*. The Post. http://projects.thepostathens.com/SpecialProjects/lgbtq-issue-2018/marginalized-groups-within-LGBTQ-umbrella.html

Salmon, J., & Quay, G. (2021, February 17). When Economic Policy Gets Woke, People Get Hurt. *Discourse*. https://www.discoursemagazine.com/economics/2021/02/16/when-economic-policy-gets-woke-people-get-hurt/

Sanzi, E. (2022, April 26). Parents are sounding the alarm on woke education for good reason. *Restoring America*. https://www.washingtonexaminer.com/restoring-america/community-family/parents-are-sounding-the-alarm-on-woke-education-for-good-reason

Sargent, G. (2023, May 25). Target's surrender to MAGA rage shows how anti-wokeness really works. *The Washington Post*. https://www.washingtonpost.com/opinions/2023/05/25/target-pulls-lgbtq-clothing-right-wing-maga/

Schambra, W. A. (2023, June 12). *The Progressive Movement and the Transformation of American Politics*. https://www.heritage.org/political-process/report/the-progressive-movement-and-the-transformation-american-politics

Schulte, G. (2021, July 17). Poll: One-third of voters identify as 'woke'. *The Hill*. https://thehill.com/hilltv/what-americas-thinking/563415-poll-one-third-of-voters-identify-as-woke/

Schwab, K. (2019). *Davos Manifesto 2020: The Universal Purpose of a Company in the Fourth Industrial Revolution*. World Economic Forum. https://www.weforum.org/agenda/2019/12/davos-manifesto-2020-the-universal-purpose-of-a-company-in-the-fourth-industrial-revolution/

Schwab, K. (2020, October 22). A Better Economy Is Possible. But We Need to Reimagine Capitalism to Do It. *Time*. https://time.com/collection/great-reset/5900748/klaus-schwab-capitalism/

Sheth, S. (2017, April 30). Bret Stephens' article on climate change costs New York Times subscribers. *Insider*. https://www.businessinsider.com/bret-stephens-new-york-times-climate-change-article-subscriptions-canceled-op-ed-2017-4

Smith, S. (2021). *Five Days After Attack, Andy Ngo Releases Statement Confirming He Was Chased and Beaten in Portland*. Willamette Week. https://www.wweek.com/

news/2021/06/02/five-days-after-attack-andy-ngo-releases-statement-confirming-he-was-chased-and-beaten-in-portland/

Smithsonian Folksways Collection. (2015). *Lead Belly: "Scottsboro Boys"*. YouTube. The Smithsonian Folksways Collection. https://www.youtube.com/watch?v=VrXfkPViFIE

Sollee, K. (2015). *6 Things To Know About 4th Wave Feminism.* Bustle. https://www.bustle.com/articles/119524-6-things-to-know-about-4th-wave-feminism

Spangler, T. (2023, January 13). Netflix Founder Reed Hastings Grants $20 Million to Minerva University. *Variety*. https://variety.com/2023/digital/news/netflix-reed-hastings-grant-minerva-university-1235487161/

Spry, A., Vredenburg, J., Kemper, J., & Kapitan, S. (2022, August 4). *Woke washing: what happens when marketing communications don't match corporate practice.* https://theconversation.com/woke-washing-what-happens-when-marketing-communications-dont-match-corporate-practice-108035

Starbucks. (2021). *The Starbucks Foundation announces nonprofit recipients of grants to support BIPOC youth.* Starbucks Foundation. https://stories.starbucks.com/press/2021/the-starbucks-foundation-announces-nonprofit-recipients-of-grants-to-support-bipoc-youth/

Stein, J. (2019, February 23). Three 2020 Democrats say 'yes' to race-based reparations — but remain vague on details. *The Washington Post*. https://www.washingtonpost.com/us-policy/2019/02/22/candidates-say-yes-race-based-reparations-remain-vague-details/

Stollznow, K. (2022, August 5). *'Virtue signalling', a slur meant to imply moral grandstanding that might not be all bad.* https://theconversation.com/virtue-signalling-a-slur-meant-to-imply-moral-grandstanding-that-might-not-be-all-bad-145546

Sunrise Movement. (2023). *Sunrise's Principles - Sunrise Movement.* Sunrise Movement. https://www.sunrisemovement.org/principles/?ms=Sunrise%27sPrinciples

Sunstein, C. R. (2007). Of Montreal and Kyoto: A Tale of Two Protocols. *Harvard Environmental Law Review*. https://dash.harvard.edu/handle/1/11354036

Surowiecki, J. (2023, May 26). The Hottest Trend in Investing Is Mostly a Sham. *The Atlantic*. https://www.theatlantic.com/ideas/archive/2023/05/esg-woke-investing-trend-reality/674197/

Szorenyi, A. (2022). *Judith Butler: their philosophy of gender explained.* The Conversation. https://theconversation.com/judith-butler-their-philosophy-of-gender-explained-192166

Tan, A. (2022). *To Dox or Not to Dox, that is The Question*. SSRN. https://doi.org/10.2139/ssrn.4369643

Tanenhaus, S. (2016, October 17). Rise of the Reactionary. *The New Yorker*. https://www.newyorker.com/magazine/2016/10/24/rise-of-the-reactionary

Target. (2020). *Target Commits $10 Million and Ongoing Resources for Rebuilding*

Efforts and Advancing Social Justice. Target Corporate. https://corporate.target.com/article/2020/06/commitments-rebuilding-and-social-justice

Tassin, C. (2023, November 5). More Consumers Want Brands and CEOs to Get Political. *Morning Consult*. https://pro.morningconsult.com/analysis/brands-ceos-political-survey-data

Team USA. (2022). *Diversity, Equity and Inclusion - USOPC 2021 Impact Report*. Team USA. https://2021impactreport.teamusa.org/sport-advancement/diversity-equity-and-inclusion.html#gsc.tab=0

Thompson, D. (2023, April 13). The Dangerous Rise of 'Front-Yard Politics'. *The Atlantic*. https://www.theatlantic.com/ideas/archive/2023/04/front-yard-placards-nimby-dei-refugees/673706/

Toke, N. (2022, February 9). Wokeism: What Does It Mean, Why Is It Important, And Why We Need To Support It. *Diversity for Social Impact™*. https://diversity.social/wokeism-woke-culture/?amp

Trimel, S. (2022, March 31). Educational Gag Orders Seek to Enforce Compulsory Patriotism. *PEN America*. https://pen.org/update-educational-gag-orders-seek-to-enforce-compulsory-patriotism/

Tuck, E., & Yang, W. K. (2012). Decolonization is not a metaphor. *Decolonization: Indigeneity, Education & Society*, *1*(1), 1–40.

Turchin, P. (2023). *End times: Elites, counter-elites, and the path of political disintegration*. Penguin Press.

Tyko, K. (2020). *Starbucks to tie executive pay to diversity goals as it announces mentorship program, anti-bias training requirements*. USA Today.

Tyson, A. (2023). *What the data says about Americans' views of climate change*. Pew Research Center. https://www.pewresearch.org/short-reads/2023/04/18/for-earth-day-key-facts-about-americans-views-of-climate-change-and-renewable-energy/

UCSUSA. (2023). *History*. Union of Concerned Scientists. https://www.ucsusa.org/about/history

Umeadi, C. (2016). *The Rise of Pseudo Intellectualism*. Medium. Umeadi, C 2016, The Rise if Pseudo Intellectualism.

United Nations. (2023). *Universal Declaration of Human Rights*. United Nations. https://www.un.org/en/about-us/universal-declaration-of-human-rights

US House of Representatives. (2023). *Rights and Representation*. US House of Representatives. https://history.house.gov/Exhibitions-and-Publications/BAIC/Historical-Essays/Keeping-the-Faith/Civil-Rights-Movement/

Vaughan, A. (2010, May 11). C4's What the Green Movement Got Wrong: environmentalists respond. *The Guardian*. https://www.theguardian.com/environment/blog/2010/nov/04/c4-what-green-movement-wrong

Vogels, E. A. (2022, June 10). *A growing share of Americans are familiar with 'cancel culture'*. https://www.pewresearch.org/short-reads/2022/06/09/a-growing-share-of-americans-are-familiar-with-cancel-culture/

Waldman, P. (2017, April 26). America's endless cycle of reactionary politics. *The*

Week. https://theweek.com/articles/694540/americas-endless-cycle-reactionary-politics

Walmart. (2021). *The Walmart.org Center for Racial Equity Awards Over $14 Million in First Round of Grants*. Walmart Corporate. https://corporate.walmart.com/newsroom/2021/02/01/the-walmart-org-center-for-racial-equity-awards-over-14-million-in-first-round-of-grants

Warzel, C. (2023, April 22). Elon Musk's Lasting Twitter Legacy. *The Atlantic*. https://www.theatlantic.com/technology/archive/2023/04/musk-twitter-shame-amplification/673814/

Washington, B. E. (2018, May 30). Starbucks After Anti-Bias Training: Will It Last? *Gallup*. https://www.gallup.com/workplace/235139/starbucks-anti-bias-training-last.aspx

Watson, E. C. (2017, February 11). The Origin Of Woke: William Melvin Kelley Is The 'Woke' Godfather We Never Acknowledged. *Okayplayer*. https://www.okayplayer.com/culture/woke-history-origins.html

Watson, E. C. (2018, February 28). The Origin Of Woke: How Erykah Badu And Georgia Anne Muldrow Sparked The "Stay Woke" Era. *Okayplayer*. https://www.okayplayer.com/originals/stay-woke-history-georgia-anne-muldrow-erykah-badu-master-teacher.html

Watson, E. C. (2020, February 26). The Origin Of Woke: How The Death Of Woke Led To The Birth Of Cancel Culture. *Okayplayer*. https://www.okayplayer.com/culture/woke-cancel-culture-history-meaning.html

Webster, S. (2022). *BLM vs. Black Panthers: What's the Difference?* What I Can Do. https://whaticando.co/blm-vs-black-panthers-whats-the-difference/

Weiss, B. (2021). *We Got Here Because of Cowardice. We Get Out With Courage - Bari Weiss, Commentary Magazine*. Commentary. https://www.commentary.org/articles/bari-weiss/resist-woke-revolution/

West, L. (2021). *J. Luke Wood Discusses Schools, Suspensions & Our Black Children*. The San Diego Voice & Viewpoint. https://sdvoice.info/j-luke-wood-discusses-schools-suspensions-our-black-children/

Whistle, W. (2020, January 1). Wealth Inequality And Higher Education: How Billionaires Could Make A Difference. *Forbes*. https://www.forbes.com/sites/wesleywhistle/2020/12/31/wealth-inequality-and-higher-education-how-billionaires-could-make-a-difference/?sh=20598cbc39db

Wike, R. (2023, June 2). *In U.S. and elsewhere, most say their country will be better off embracing changes over sticking to traditions*. https://www.pewresearch.org/short-reads/2023/05/15/in-us-and-elsewhere-most-say-their-country-will-be-better-off-embracing-changes-over-sticking-to-traditions/

Williams, C. (2021). *For Those With an Opinion on ESG, Environmentally Friendly Investing Is Top of Mind*. Morning Consult. https://pro.morningconsult.com/articles/esg-investments-environmental-issues-poll

Williams, J. (2021). *How woke conquered the world*. CIEO. https://www.cieo.org.uk/research/how-woke-conquered-the-world/

Williams, J. (2022). *How woke won: The elitist movement that threatens democracy, tolerance and reason / Joanna Williams* (First edition). John Wilkes.

Willis, R. (2022). *What is Rainbow Capitalism and what can we do about it.* Outpatch. https://outpatch.org/blogs/stories/rainbowcapitalism

Wolla, S., & Sullivan, J. (2017). *Education Income And Wealth.* Federal Reserve Bank of St Louis. https://research.stlouisfed.org/publications/page1-econ/2017/01/03/education-income-and-wealth/

Women's March. (2022). *Our Feminist Future.* Women's March. https://www.womensmarch.com/

Yearby, R., Clark, B., & Figueroa, J. F. (2022). Structural Racism In Historical And Modern US Health Care Policy. *Health Affairs (Project Hope)*, *41*(2), 187–194. https://doi.org/10.1377/hlthaff.2021.01466

Zero Hour. (2023). *Who We Are — This Is Zero Hour.* Zero Hour. https://www.thisiszerohour.org/whoweare

Zwaagstra, M. (2022). *Pushing Woke Ideology in Schools.* Frontier Centre For Public Policy. https://fcpp.org/2022/09/23/pushing-woke-ideology-in-schools/

ABOUT THE AUTHOR

Nina Thom wears many hats—holding a Master's degree in Cultural Heritage, she's a seasoned Psychotherapist, a tireless advocate for social justice, and the accomplished author behind "Woke or Not? A Guide to Woke for Older People."

Nina's exploration of Wokeism mirrors that of many in her generation, sparked by thought-provoking conversations with her adult children. These dialogues plunged her into the rapidly evolving currents of change, inspiring a profound investigation into the controversial realm of woke culture. Driven by her desire to shed light on these intricate concepts, she embarked on a mission to impart her insights to fellow parents and those grappling to grasp these ideas.

With an impressive three-decade career, Nina's academic pursuits have centered on researching cultural frameworks within minority communities. As an experienced Psychotherapist in a private clinic, she has extended her commitment to healing by aiding those who've endured trauma and abuse. Presently, her endeavors encompass managing Volunteer groups and championing legal reforms within the social justice landscape. Nina's dedication extends to her role as a board member governing multiple non-profit organizations.

Although semi-retired in a quiet rural enclave, Nina's life is far from confined. Alongside her feline companion Toby, she finds joy in refurbishing her mid-century home, living close to mountains and lakes, and finding the best coffee in town.

Amidst her travels locally and abroad, she's embraced the digital realm and the power of online video platforms to bridge geographical divides and maintain connections with friends and family scattered across the globe.

Printed in Dunstable, United Kingdom

71497789R00111